Courtyard Gardens

Courtyard Gardens
imaginative ideas for outdoor living

Toby Musgrave

jacqui small

For Aulani.
Thank you for bringing so much to my life.

First published in 2000 by Jacqui Small
an imprint of Aurum Press Ltd
25 Bedford Avenue
London WC1B 3AT

2005 2004 2003 2002 2001
10 9 8 7 6 5 4 3 2

Text and courtyard designs copyright
© Toby Musgrave 2000
Illustration, design and layout copyright
© Jacqui Small 2000

Publisher **Jacqui Small**
Editorial consultant **Erica Hunningher**
Editor **Casey Horton**
Designer **Maggie Town**
Illustrator **Helen Smythe**
Picture researcher **Emily Hedges**
Courtyard design **Toby Musgrave**
Production **Geoff Barlow**

British Library
Cataloguing-in-Publication Data:
A catalogue record for this book is
available from the British Library

ISBN 1 903 221 01 3

Printed and bound in China

Photographs on pages 1 to 5:
Page 1
An open gateway provides an entrance to a
tranquil and secluded space. This is the very
essence of a courtyard garden – a hide-away,
a piece of paradise on Earth.

Page 2
The small, regularly shaped courtyard
appears larger and less geometric as a result of
the judicious positioning of large, architecturally
shaped plants. The intimate space evokes an
atmosphere of romance, which is heightened
by the privacy afforded by the overhanging tree.

Page 3
Strong forms and shapes are characteristic
of the knot garden, a traditional form of hedging
that brings a sense of stability, permanence and
timelessness to a courtyard.

This page
A change in level gives this tiny courtyard an
added dimension and prevents it from appearing
too long and narrow. The boundaries are blurred
further by an admixture of eclectic ornaments
and a choice variety of plants, all of which create
a sense of purpose and individuality.

contents

the art
of courtyard gardening

A courtyard provides a place of refuge in which to retreat from the rest of the world. This has always been so, for the courtyard garden is as old as garden making itself. By deciding to create a courtyard garden of your own, you are carrying on an ancient and respected tradition, one that began at least 5,000 years ago.

Ancient Egyptian tomb paintings depict the first courtyard gardens as sanctuaries, open to the sky and enclosed by walls or palisades that gave protection from marauders and the hot desert winds. Within these walls were shady, verdant oases where rectangular pools, fed with water from the Nile, were edged with flowerbeds and shaded by tall trees and vine-clad pergolas – an island of tranquillity and spiritual refreshment.

Down the centuries, the style of courtyard design (which, in part, is dependent on the prevailing climate and available plants) has varied from country to country and changed with time. Yet the very popularity of the courtyard garden has ensured that there is now a rich, global legacy of garden making ideas, which can be used to solve modern design dilemmas in all manner of interesting and intriguing ways.

The tradition of courtyard gardening continues today as the perfect solution for creating an extension to the home. It offers greater scope for outdoor living than simply building a conservatory or a glazed garden room, and its potential is not limited by its size. As well as providing a place of beauty and restfulness, a room outside is somewhere to entertain and cultivate plants, a corner in which to refresh the mind and revitalize the spirit.

In order to create a courtyard that reflects your lifestyle and personality, and meets your aesthetic needs, time and budget, a well-thought-out design and careful planning are essential. Approached as a sequential set of tasks, this can be an enjoyable and rewarding process, providing you with the opportunity to express your creative spirit at each stage, and a great sense of achievement once the tasks have been completed. Before you do anything, establish precisely what you want and decide on the style of the courtyard. Ask yourself what its purpose is to be, and how you want it to look. It can be formal or informal, designed along historical lines or incorporating elements from different periods and cultures. By looking to the past and adapting a design suitable for a modern lifestyle, you will enjoy the novelty and excitement of bringing history to life and creating a garden that is relevant, affordable, attainable and a little out of the ordinary.

Study the designs in Style Sources (pages 14-52) which offers ten three-dimensional garden plans complete with detailed descriptions and comprehensive lists of plantings and materials employed. The plans have been inspired by courtyard garden styles from the past – ancient Rome through Europe and Japan to the Americas – and include a glance into the future. However, you need not restrict yourself to an historical style. Courtyards can be designed to meet a specific theme or purpose – romantic, easy to maintain, a place to entertain guests and so on. A further eight designs, styled along these lines, can be found in Designing by Theme (pages 56-90).

Having chosen a theme or style, decide on the framework features – those items and materials that establish the shape, layout and mood. Some of the ever-increasing range of materials and furnishings

A strong and well planned design (opposite) that utilizes a range of complementary materials is essential in creating an overall feeling of space well used.

The geometric pattern (above right) of box hedging emphasizes the symmetrical pattern of the courtyard, which is edged with brick. This parterre demonstrates how relevant traditional elements can be to the modern courtyard designer. It also illustrates how the design should take into consideration views within the garden.

Enclosure provides privacy (centre right), and where it forms part of the garden's framework, it should be attractive. Focal features, such as sculpture, are essential, as they draw the eye to specific points in the garden, while trees cast cool dappled shade.

Planting softens the hard landscaping (bottom right) and vertical structures, while the mirror in the trellis work shelter provides an optical illusion, adding an element of surprise and, possibly, momentary confusion.

for the structural elements of the courtyard are described in The Framework (pages 94-120). The type of boundary and any internal divisions need to be chosen to match the overall style, as do the plants and paving materials. Decide whether or not you want water and, if so, in what form – tinkling rills for relaxation, a spouting fountain for excitement or a calm, limpid pool to reflect the sky.

Lighting is another important element for consideration, and should be planned from the outset, as electric cables have to be installed early in the building process. Architectural plants, some of which might already be in situ if you are transforming an existing garden, add living structure and are useful for providing a link between the house and the garden.

The features and effects that furnish your courtyard must also be chosen to match the overall style. Sculpture, containers, shading and furniture heighten the mood, increase interest and introduce ornamentation. For each garden style there are many different ornamental elements that can be included, all of which are dealt with in Decorative Features and Effects (pages 124-136).

The third stage in creating your garden is to work with a scale drawing of your courtyard, made on tracing paper. If it is to be a completely new garden, then this piece of paper will show little more than the shape of the plot, doors from the house, north-south orientation, and any views beyond the garden that might be exploited by apertures in boundaries. Orientation will reveal sunny and shady areas of the plot and will influence where you site your sitting area or water feature. Note, too, any slopes that might need to be transformed into a flight of steps, or areas that could be excavated to create a

Asymmetry and bold architectural forms (right) are the basic elements in this modern courtyard. The design both reflects and contrasts with the landscape beyond, incorporating the natural forms of plant and stone with cast concrete and an artificial watercourse.

Decoratively patterned floor and wall tiles (below) contribute to the elegance of of this Islamic-influenced courtyard. This is a low-maintenance garden, perfect for relaxing – as the cat so conveniently demonstrates.

pond. If you are remaking an existing garden, you should mark on the plan the position of any plants and features you want to retain.

With the outlines mapped out, play around with a soft pencil and eraser, fitting the new features and ornaments into the space in a unified way. As part of this process, remember that you will be creating views from the house windows.

Resolving the practical aspects will make the garden fall into place. If you have thought about how you will move around the space (paths and steps) and how you will use it, your courtyard will be well proportioned and will feel restful and calm. If you stamp it with your own individuality, you will know when the arrangement looks right.

The final step is to plan the planting. Keep in mind the old adage 'right plant, right place', and select plants that will survive in the climate and grow in your soil (the latter requirement can be mitigated by using pots), otherwise you will fight a losing battle. Dig two or three holes to test the depth of the top soil. If it is less than 30cm, you should increase the depth by importing top soil. If your soil is heavy clay, you will need to improve it by incorporating organic manure and washed sand, and if you live in an area of high rainfall, consider installing subsoil drainage. Use a soil-testing kit to test the soil pH (less than 7 is acid, 7 is neutral, and above 7 is alkaline) and look at the plants that are growing well in neighbouring gardens.

For a catalogue of plants suitable for courtyards, see Plants for Courtyard Gardens (pages 142-155), which provides profiles of more than 400 plants, arranged by use. This will make selecting the right plant for the right place that much more straightforward. However, if you want to be purist when creating an historically influenced design,

remember that you should use only period correct plants – species that were available at that time.

When you have your plan on paper you are ready to build, but it is wise to think the project through and construct a work schedule that breaks the task into stages. Begin with the hard landscaping, such as walls, raised beds, paving, paths and water features; then move to the ornaments and features and finish with the planting. For certain jobs you will need professional help, but for the rest, have a go yourself. If you make the occasional mistake, think of it as part of the process of arriving at the right solution. When it is complete, you can stand back with pride and know you have created your own piece of paradise – an apt word, derived from the Old Persian, *pairidaeza*, meaning 'a walled space'.

The Mediterranean-style courtyard (left) relies to a large extent on the use of container plants and hard surfaces. Here dark green foliage provides a rich contrast to deep pink walls.

Architectural plants (below) can be positioned to draw attention to particular parts of the courtyard garden. To achieve this, either plant contrasting species or use large, individual specimens.

There is no need to give the whole courtyard over to crops to reap their ornamental rewards. Mixing fruit and vegetables with ornamental species can be as spectacular as it is unusual. Begin by training fruit trees into different shapes against the walls, making certain that nectarine, fig and peach are against a warm, sunny boundary. You can also make delightful wall coverings from scramblers such as blackberries or vines. In beds and borders, fruit bushes make excellent feature plants, while the scarlet flowers and fresh green foliage of runner beans makes a wonderful backdrop or a temporary hedge. Herbs will fit in anywhere. The roundness of cabbages, the crinkly red leaves of lollo rossa and fluffy foliage of carrots add different textures to a flowerbed. *Solanaceae* – tomatoes (red, green and yellow), peppers, chillies, aubergine – all add a splash of colour.

The graceful *Cynara cardunculus* (cardoon), a relative of the artichoke, has exotic foliage and electric blue flowers, and makes a splash in any herbaceous border. Many cucurbits – gourds, marrows, courgettes, and so on – with striking leaves, bright flowers and outlandish fruit, can be used as exotic ground cover or as features grown over a support. On the smallest scale, a hanging basket planted with herbs or trailing tomatoes can be added to an ornamental garden.

The plan overleaf combines beauty with utility – a formal ornamental layout full of crops. Around the walls, whitewashed to reflect light and heat into the garden, fruit trees are trained as fans, espaliers and cordons, shapes that are pieces of art in their own right. The small circular beds near the house are dedicated to soft fruit trees (blackcurrant and gooseberry) and strawberries, and flank a space for a table and chairs, where you can sit alfresco and admire your hard work or eat its results. The matching beds at the other end of the garden are planted with summer salad crops. In the winter and spring these could be planted with seasonal bedding to fill the bare soil and add a dash of colour. This plan is not a blueprint, and these beds could be planted with different crops, or even perhaps flowers for cutting, with *Lathyrus odorata* (sweet pea) replacing the runner beans and cucumber on the ornamental tepee frames.

The central circle with its raised beds and maze pattern paving slab is designed to look interesting. The posts and ropes add height and structure, and could be planted with climbers such as climbing roses, jasmine, clematis or honeysuckle, or fruit crops such as blackberry or loganberry, or a mixture of both. The four quarters are given over to vegetables and herbs. They are an easy size to maintain but there is a practical reason for four beds. Growing the same crops in the same place year after year can cause soil nutrition deficiencies and a build-up of pests and diseases. To minimize problems, a four-year crop rotation programme is used. Each bed is planted with a single crop group, and at the end of each growing season the crops are moved one bed to the left (or right). This means that at the start of the fifth season you are back where you began. The table below lists the four crop groups with a few examples.

The foliage montage (above) of several brassicas is a study in exciting and exotic shapes, textures and colours. The frothy leaves and white flowers of *Cosmos* help to lighten the display.

Mixing and matching (opposite) creates an unusual design. The ironwork pillars are covered with scarlet runner beans and sweet peas, which blend perfectly with the underplanted begonias and strawberries.

Herbs (below), irrespective of their planting arrangements and associations, never fail to look attractive – especially; when combined with ornamental perennials.

Legumes & Pods	Alliums	Solanaceous	Brassicas
broad beans, French and runner beans, lima beans, dolchas beans, peanuts, peas, okra	bulb onions, spring onions, shallots, leeks, garlic, European onions, Welsh onions	tomatoes, sweet peppers, aubergine, celery, celeriac	pak choi, cauliflower, cabbage, Brussels sprouts, purple sprouting broccoli, kohl rabi, Chinese cabbage

plants for an edible courtyard

1 Peach (*Prunus persica*) **2** Fig (*Ficus carica*)

3 Red runner bean (*Phaseolus coccineus*)

4 Cucumber (*Cucumis sativus*) **5** Pear (*Pyrus communis*) **6** Lettuce (*Lactuca sativa*) 'Cos'

7 Lettuce (*Lactuca sativa*) 'Lollo Rosso'

8 Lettuce (*Lactuca sativa*) 'Butterhead'

9 Spinach (*Spinacia oleracea*) **10** Salad rocket (*Eruca vesicaria*) **11** Tomato (*Lycopersicon esculentum*) **12** Radish (*Raphanus sativus*)

13 Bulb and spring onion (*Allium cepa*) **14** Apricot (*Prunus armeniaca*) **15** Apple (*Malus domestica*)

16 Parsnip (*Pastinaca sativa*) **17** Carrot (*Daucus carota*) **18** Potato (*Solanum tuberosum*) **19** Basil (*Ocimum basilicum*) **20** Greek oregano (*Origanum vulgare* ssp. *hirtum*) **21** Turnip (*Brassica rapa* Rapifera Group) **22** Brussels sprout (*Brassica oleracea* Gemmifera Group) **23** Cabbage (*Brassica oleracea* Capitata Group) **24** Parsley (*Petroselinum crispum*) **25** Garden thyme (*Thymus vulgaris*)

26 Broad bean (*Vicia faba*) **27** Pea (*Pisum sativum*)

28 French bean (*Phaseolus vulgaris*)

29 Peppermint (*Mentha* x *piperita*) **30** Dill (*Anethum graveolens*) **31** Plum (*Prunus domestica*)

32 Garlic (*Allium sativum*) **33** Leek (*Allium porrum*)

34 Coriander (*Coriandrum sativum*) **35** Marjoram (*Origanum majorana*) **36** Strawberry (*Fragaria* x *ananassa*) **37** Blackcurrant (*Ribes nigrum*)

38 Gooseberry (*Ribes uva-crispa*)

This courtyard will provide a wide range of fruit and vegetables in season, but if you want early crops, you may want to make space for a greenhouse and/or a cold frame, sited in a sunny spot. However, regardless of whether you give your whole garden over to food crops, or just integrate a few plants into your existing garden, the scope for inventive and attractive gardening with edible crops is enormous. Whatever you grow will bring satisfaction and achievement when you sit down to eat your home-grown produce – and, perhaps a slight smugness knowing you have also saved yourself money; home grown is cheaper than the supermarket.

This formal herb garden (top left) has a hint of the knot garden about it, and imparts a Renaissance feel, emphasized by the old cauldrons used as pots. In addition to being very pretty, the bed is low maintenance, as there is no bare soil in which weeds could get a foothold.

The decaying wall (left), with its unusual texture and colour, is a striking backdrop for this harmonious display of herbs. The carpeting mounds of thyme species, the purple sage and the upright angelica all stand apart, yet blend together in perfect harmony.

entertaining ideas

A courtyard that provides space for entertaining is two gardens in one – a place in which to enjoy a meal with family and friends, and a quiet garden to delight in on your own once everyone has left. With careful planning, taking into consideration the comfort of your guests as well as your own, you will be able to create a garden that adequately fulfils these conditions.

A place for alfresco entertaining is a room outside, comprising walls, a floor, furniture and decoration, where the ceiling is the sky. Successful entertaining requires the right ambience – a welcoming atmosphere in a comfortable space. Consider the way in which people and objects interact, and work out how much space each feature needs in relation to the average person. As in your dining room, for example, a chair at a table needs enough space to be pulled out, and you have to be able to move around it and sit down without bumping into your neighbour.

Scented plants, soft lighting and music and comfortable seating – whether wooden chairs, wrought iron seats, stone benches, or just rugs and cushions scattered on the ground – set the mood for relaxed entertaining. And if you wish to eat outside, the table can be a decorative feature in its own right or a more simple, portable, one that can be folded up and stored when not in use.

For comfort, awnings, umbrellas, canopies, or trees will protect guests from harsh sun and rain. Lighting is another essential and, for subtle effects, candles are a good option, especially those that repel insects. If you are hardy and want to be outside in cooler

Friendly and welcoming (right), this sheltered dining area is a place in which visitors will instinctively feel at home. The table is positioned to take advantage of the view, while the aquamarine pool is as enticing as it is cool.

Protected from the heat of the sun (below) by the tiled roof, wooden benches furnished with soft cushions offer a place to sit, relax and entertain guests. The serving counter-cum-bar in the corner is a particularly civilized addition, avoiding the need to keep returning to the house for provisions.

A double avenue of trees (right) defines the dining area and provides a shady canopy of foliage. The garden is made to feel much larger by the cunning use of a mirror, placed to face the table, which is an imposing feature in its own right.

A profusion of exotic foliage (opposite right) encloses a secret hide-away in which to enjoy al fresco meals. The wooden furniture, simple but attractive, has weathered gently so that it matches the wooden decking that elevates the area.

A scattering of vibrant coloured cushions (left) and a bright painted wall provide striking contrasts to the more subdued colours of cane and wood. There is more than a hint of the tropics in this courtyard design, which is suitably enhanced by the bold architectural planting.

A small corner (above) provides an intimate setting for an outdoor dining room. The backdrop of deep green ivy is the perfect foil for the black wrought-iron furniture, while the wall light and candles make dining after dark a possibility.

Texture and pattern (opposite) make a considerable contribution to the elegant formality of this courtyard garden (seen also on page 9). Glass tabletops not only increase the amount of available light but also provide reflective surfaces that mingle the brickwork beneath with the greenery and sky overhead.

weather, you may want to install a gas heater. Space is often at a premium, so features for entertaining may need to have a dual role. A functional concrete seat could also be a piece of art; a marble table could be a stand for pot plants as well as a place for serving food; built-in seats can have hinged lids for storage; and herbs are ornamental and provide fragrance as well as being edible.

The plants, while beautiful in their own right, can also serve as a welcoming feature. Those near the seating and dining areas should preferably have strongly perfumed flowers, but choose species that bloom when you are using the garden most – perhaps fragrant roses in the summer, or in a hot climate, in the evening, *Matthiola longipetala* (night-scented stock) or the deliciously scented *Nicotiana* (tobacco plant). Unusual plants can be used as a lure and, when placed at a distance, will be an invitation to explore other areas of the courtyard.

The plan shows a courtyard that has been designed for a range of entertaining activities. Immediately outside the door into the garden is the cooking and dining area, and away to the left is an area of lawn for relaxation. To unify the two areas and help instil a calm atmosphere, the walls are painted a soft rose pink.

The colour theme of the flowers is white, soft blue, reds and pink, with the occasional eye-catcher such as *Potentilla fruticosa* 'Red Ace', *Taxus baccata* 'Fastigiata' and *Cornus florida*. Many of the species also have scented flowers or foliage, such as *Lavandula* (lavender), which you brush past when leaving or entering the house, and *Rosa* 'Indigo'. The rose-pink theme is picked up in the dining area. The table is surrounded by a ring of pink granite setts with radiating spokes that lead to four pink granite pots planted with herbs. The other two colours are repeated in the white granite setts of the floor, and in the dazzling white bark of the four birch trees – *Betula utilis* var. *jacquemontii* 'Silver Shadow' – that shade the dining table during the day and provide a leafy canopy through which the stars twinkle at night. A thick glass table, which appears ice blue, provides the focal point in the dining area.

To complete the colour matching and unify the garden, one of the twin arched bowers at either end of the garden is covered in white wisteria and surrounded with white lavender; the other is blue. The cooking station against the far wall features a barbecue and a beehive terracotta oven with associated workspace. Once the entertaining is over, all the paraphernalia – the collapsible chairs, the cushions and rugs and cooking equipment – can be stored out of the way in the dry wooden boxes beneath the seats in the arches.

plants for an entertaining courtyard

1 *Taxus baccata* 'Fastigiata'

2 *Iris* 'Carnaby' **3** *Iris* 'Early Light'

4 *Iris* 'Flamenco' **5** *Iris* 'Stepping Out'

6 *Rosa* 'Coral Dawn'

7 *Monarda* 'Croftway Pink'

8 *Potentilla fruticosa* 'Red Ace'

9 *Hemerocallis* 'Stafford'

10 *Laurus nobilis*

11 *Origanum vulgare*

12 *Betula utilis* var. *jacquemontii* 'Silver Shadow'

13 *Ocimum basilicum*

14 *Rosa gallica* var. *officinalis* 'Versicolor'

15 *Nicotiana alata*

16 *Lavandula angustifolia* 'Alba'

17 *Wisteria sinensis* 'Alba'

18 *Cornus florida*

19 *Convolvulus tricolor*

20 *Allium schoenoprasum*

21 *Thymus vulgaris*

22 *Lavandula angustifolia*

23 *Nepeta x faassenii*

24 *Rosa* 'Indigo'

25 *Delphinium* 'Blue Nile'

26 *Lilium regale*

27 *Wisteria sinensis*

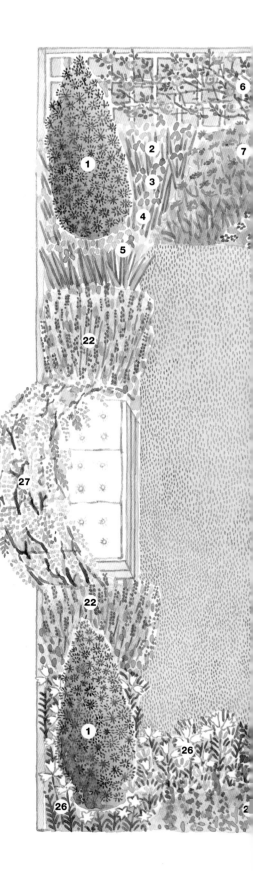

the spa
treatment

The spa garden is dedicated to relaxing and entertaining. It is a place to enjoy a range of pleasurable and health-giving treatments within an attractive garden framework that can be tailored to suit all tastes and climates. With careful planning the courtyard will successfully marry the practical with the decorative.

The spa courtyard can be created and enjoyed anywhere – a night time soak in the bubbling warmth of a hot tub when the ground is covered in snow is as pleasant as a midday, post-sauna cold plunge when it is 38°C in the shade. It is a very congenial style, as it encourages friends, neighbours and family to drop by, enjoy a spa, chat and unwind. And because planting can be kept to a minimum, it requires little maintenance.

Treatments – sauna, hot tub, steam room, cold plunge pool and shower, dominate the spa courtyard, but it is also a garden. Therefore, your design needs to be dual purpose: decide on the treatments you want to enjoy and on the style of garden within which you wish to arrange them. This offers great freedom of choice, as spa treatments will meld easily with many garden styles. Where winters are cold, a Scandinavian atmosphere is appropriate: white-painted walls, wooden decking floors (from an environmentally sustainable source), sheltered corners and

architectural planting will combine to create a traditional feel. For a Japanese flavour, clad the walls with bamboo screens and make a small Zen rock and gravel garden, an approach that would also work well in areas with low rainfall. For a modern ambience, dyed concrete floors, mirrors on the walls and stainless steel planters make an impact; and if you want a more informal, floral garden, simply set the treatment centres among flowerbeds and lawn. However, to minimize the amount of dirt getting into the various treatment centres, avoid the necessity of walking on loose flooring materials such as sand, gravel or bark chips.

Once you have decided on treatments and style, the next stage is to integrate the two elements. Practicality is essential and the treatment centres should be easily accessible from the house and

A bubbling hot tub (opposite left), hidden away among exotic foliage, is as alluring on a warm summer's day as on a cold winter's evening.

Ornamental grasses (left) have been thoughtfully planted to provide an attractive living screen, which ensures the pool area and bathers are not overlooked.

The electric blue (above) of this plunge pool contrasts strongly but effectively with the terracotta tile floor. The asymmetric shape of the pool successfully breaks up the rectangular shape of the courtyard, while the planting blurs the edges. Both techniques help make the space feel larger than it is.

from each other. However, rather than being crowded together, they should be arranged in such a way that there are usable spaces between them. These spaces then become home to the screened off, secluded areas for sitting and cooling off, open areas for entertaining, the beds/borders and ornamental garden features, such as sculpture. As the courtyard will be used at night, the final task is to position the lights for easy movement around the garden as well as dramatic effect.

Beds provide an effective setting for the treatment centres and, if planted with sufficiently large plants, create visual blocks, thereby separating the courtyard into a series of experiences and increasing intimacy. To enjoy maximum relaxation and minimal maintenance, use a mixed planting of shrubs, herbaceous species and bulbs. To keep matters even less labour intensive, plant architectural specimen shrubs such as *Corylus avellana* 'Contorta', *Salix babylonica* 'Tortuosa' or *Fremontodendron californicum* set within ground cover plants or a mulch of gravel or stone chips. If you have decided on a plunge pool, why not ornament it with a bog garden planted with marginals such as candelabra *Primula* species, *Hosta*, *Fillipendula*, and the spectacular *Zantedeschia aethiopica*. To prevent soil escaping into the pool, ensure the bed is self-contained. To add another low-maintenance, artistic dimension, augment the beds with specimen plants in planters or large pots, and remember that, irrespective of the effect you decide on, plants look fantastic at night if carefully lit.

The plan shows a design influenced by Scandinavian traditions and planted primarily with Chinese and Japanese architectural evergreen specimen shrubs. The perimeter boundary is a white-painted closeboard fence, and wood and white dominate the courtyard. Near the house is the wooden decking seating-cum-entertaining area. The decking is raised 15cm above ground level to allow drainage and air circulation; below the decking the ground is concrete or soil covered, with a permeable polypropylene membrane to suppress weed growth. The flat decking is sheltered by the uplit *Betula populifolia* (grey birch) and an awning which can be extended for increased privacy.

White granite rocks, a bed of marginal plants and stainless steel planters soften the decking and introduce height. Moving forward, the asymmetrical plunge pool divides the garden, while the narrowing decking draws you through the gateway created by container-grown mahonia into the further half of the garden.

In this half of the garden, surrounded by plants and accessed by decking stepping stones set in white granite chips, are the sauna constructed from a large redwood barrel, and the hot tub, reached by climbing up two steps to the decking surround. The mixture of evergreen shrubs and ground cover, many of which flower and introduce seasonal variety, are features in their own right, but they also help to soften the layout and separate the treatments, creating the feeling that the garden is larger than it is.

plants for a spa courtyard

1 *Viola odorata*

2 *Tradescantia virginiana* (white)

3 *Magnolia stellata*

4 *Euonymus fortunei* 'Emerald 'n' Gold'

5 *Chaenomeles japonica*

6 *Phyllostachys bambusoide* 'Allgold'

7 *Prunus subhirtella* 'Autumnalis'

8 *Camellia* x *williamsii* 'Donation'

9 *Hamamelis mollis*

10 *Mahonia aquifolium* 'Apollo'

11 *Phyllostachys nigra* var. *henonis*

12 *Pinus mugo*

13 *Pleioblastus variegatus*

14 *Convallaria majalis*

15 *Euonymus fortuneii* 'Silver Queen'

16 *Chaenomeles speciosa*

17 *Mahonia japonica*

18 *Hakonechloa macra* 'Aureola'

19 *Betula populifolia*

20 *Phormium tenax* Purpureum Group

21 *Rubus tricolor*

22 *Dicksonia antarctica*

23 *Primula vialii*

24 *Hosta ventricosa*

25 *Matteuccia struthiopteris*

The angular shape of the pool (left) is defined by stone paving, which beautifully complements the blue tiles. There is a feeling of movement and vigour in this design.

Wooden decking (far left), the wooden dividing wall and the raised wooden hot tub give this balcony garden a very organic look. This is picked up and emphasized by the earthenware pots, stone edging and the architectural planting. The position of the hot tub allows views over the steel and glass boundary.

For natural, dappled shade, plant deciduous trees at a distance from the house in order to avoid the risk of root damage, or construct a bower from trellis work or woven willow wands. Train scented climbers through the branches to heighten the sensory experience.

Tents have many advantages. They are lightweight, easy to erect and maintain (wipe the material regularly and clean thoroughly once a year), and are perfect for entertaining and relaxing. They also suit many garden styles. An Arabian Nights retreat, with pitched canvas or marine acrylic roof, brings the romance of the desert to a courtyard, while brightly coloured PVC or coated nylon supported on stainless steel poles is avant-garde. The colour of the fabric will have an impact on the ambience of the garden – neutral, creamy white is most agreeable at a distance, with dominant colours best near the house. Coloured fabrics also filter light, so choose a warm colour such as yellow to reduce glare and to brighten up cloudy days.

Awnings are available as the traditional wall-mounted type that can be wound up and down (often seen on café and shop fronts) or irregularly shaped, sail-like structures set at an angle and supported on a wall and on poles. Sails are most effective when small, with several in a row. Yet simple is often best, and the parasol on a wooden pole has a timeless elegance. It is easy to store when not in use and may be moved around the garden to bring a feeling of intimacy to dining and entertaining. Neutral coloured fabrics are best for toning down sunlight without being obtrusive.

The dappled shade (left) cast by a roof of bamboo canes is in stark contrast to the white, sun-drenched walls of the courtyard. In a hot climate a form of shading is essential to enable you to use and enjoy your garden during the heat of the day.

A charming retreat (above) has been created using a traditional way of roofing with concave tiles and supporting beams. The hollow back wall will encourage a cooling through-breeze. There is even a curtain to draw if more privacy is required.

furniture

To enjoy your personal paradise to the full, functional garden furniture must be comfortable and assigned a semi-permanent position. For example, place a sun-lounger in the corner of the garden that catches evening light, and tables and chairs for outdoor dining near the door to the house.

The colour of the furniture contributes to the mood of the courtyard garden. Natural wood, which suits all garden styles, ranges in colour from sandy pine to rich tawny cedar, and acquires an attractive patina with age (it also takes on a silvery hue as it weathers). Painted furniture makes more of a visual impact. White is bold, while green is strident if set against a foliage backdrop, and should be avoided. Choose soft pastels to complement a flowering scheme.

The style and durability of furniture lies in the choice of materials. Hardwoods, such as iroko, teak and cedar (from a sustainable source) require little maintenance – an oiling every few years is all that is usually necessary. Softwoods such as pine should be treated with stain or painted annually. Stainless steel and cast aluminium, appropriate for a modern look, need only the occasional polish. Elegant wrought iron seats, perfect for a period setting, should be checked for rust and painted every year or so. Wicker and woven willow furniture must be protected from rain. Plastic furniture, although inexpensive and requiring no maintenance, does not weather well and is never stylish. However, it is useful to have a few lightweight chairs to take into the garden as necessary. Folding furniture such as bright stripy deck chairs,

Ornate cast ironwork (left) painted green and white helps to define the ambience and style of this courtyard. It combines with the evergreen foliage, gravel flooring and clipped box to generate the timeless elegance of an Arts and Crafts garden from the end of the19th century. The white bench helps to lighten the courtyard and balance the variety of greens in the furniture and the foliage.

The rich colour (top right) of the polished wood echoes the deep tones of the tiled floor, and contrasts with the decorative terracotta pot. The bench also brings a note of tranquillity to this corner of the courtyard.

Simply elegant (right), the bench has been constructed from three pieces of cut slate, providing a place to sit, as well as a contrast to the soft planting.

A zany rocking chair (above), made from aluminium, is exactly the style of furniture needed to complement the bright colours and cheerful planting of this flamboyant garden.

The mass (left) of the stone table set of a solid base gives a sense of permanence. Slatted wooden benches balance the table, thus preventing the furniture from becoming too imposing. The table and benches have both weathered to a soft, mellow colour that matches the walls.

Ornate benches (above) can be used to introduce a sense of formality into an otherwise informally planted part of the garden.

Table and chairs (opposite, left) find a natural home beneath this raised, classically inspired, climber-clad shelter. Elevating furniture in this way will provide a different view over the courtyard, as well as creating a feature to be seen from other parts of the garden.

upright director's chairs, painted café table and chairs, or a hammock, are perfect choices where space is at a premium.

If furniture is permanently sited to play an ornamental role, materials, shapes and styles will govern your choice: a turf or chamomile seat to provide a focal point, a circular wrought iron seat around a tree trunk or concrete lounger lurking among foliage as a surprise. Seats built into retaining walls bring you closer to the planting. In some cases, comfort may be sacrificed for visual impact, but try and combine beauty and utility.

A sculpture (top right) or a seat? This modern piece, designed using clear lines and curves, has been positioned in the middle of a traditional garden to make a statement. It aptly demonstrates how, if carefully selected and positioned, furniture can fulfil a practical role as somewhere to sit, and an artistic role, as something to stimulate debate.

Perfect for a siesta (right), this lounger with its Indian-looking throw and cushions is hidden away against a wall, just waiting for someone to take a nap away from the noonday heat. Siting furniture should take into account needs of privacy and escape.

plants
for courtyard gardens

Over 400 plants, used in the designs on pages 16–93, are described in the following pages. They have been selected because they are appropriate for small gardens, and courtyards in particular. The plants are arranged in categories to help you find plants for a specific purpose: for boundaries and divisions should you want a perimeter hedge or living internal screens; to clothe pergolas and trellis, fences and walls; and as eye-catching specimens. With the framework planting in place, you can then choose plants to provide seasonal colour, foliage interest and ground cover.

Each plant description includes the Latin and common names, where applicable, and the cultivation requirements, to enable you to choose plants that suit your climate, aspect and soil. Do not feel constrained by the categories – as long as you give a plant its preferred soil type, moisture, the right amount of sun and suitable temperature, you can use the information for a number of different purposes.

Key

Light requirements

○ Full Sun

◐ Partial Shade

● Shade Loving

Moisture requirements

○ Well Drained

◗ Moist

◆ Wet

Special soil requirements
(if applicable)

<7 needs acid soil

>7 needs alkaline soil

Seasonal display

Sp Spring

Su Summer

Au Autumn

Wi Winter

Hardiness

TT Fully Tender – protect below 4°C

HH Half Hardy – can withstand temperatures to 0°C

FH Frost Hardy – can withstand temperatures to –5°C

VH Very Hardy – can withstand temperatures to –15°C

Plant size

↕ Height

•• Spread

Plant categories

Enclosure and Division

Buxus sempervirens Box
○ ◌ VH ⋮ 4.5m · · 4.5m
Evergreen bushy shrub with a mass of small, oval, glossy, dark green leaves. Ideal for hedging, edging and topiary.

Carpinus betulus
Common hornbeam
○ ◌ VH ⋮ 25m · · 20m
Deciduous tree. Grey, fluted trunk, yellow and orange leaves in autumn. Good on clay and chalk soils.

Crataegus succulenta var. macracantha Thorn
○ ◌ VH ⋮ 5m · · 5m
Deciduous tree with long thorns. Clusters of white flowers in spring followed by bright crimson fruit. Coloured leaves in autumn.

Fagus sylvatica Common beech
○ ◌ VH ⋮ 25m · · 20m
Deciduous tree with pale green leaves, later dark green, then orangey-brown in autumn. Clipped hedges retain the dead leaves throughout the winter. *F. s.* Atropurpurea Group (purple beech) has blackish-purple leaves.

Ilex aquifolium Common holly
○ ◌ VH ⋮ 20m · · 6m
Evergreen erect tree with glossy, dark green leaves with sharp spines. If pollinated, female plants have bright red berries.

Phyllostachys bambusoides 'Allgold' Bamboo
○ ◌ VH ⋮ 6-8m · · indefinite
Evergreen, clump forming, with yellow canes sometimes striped green. Creates a perfect narrow division. Remove new sideshoots to prevent spreading.

Rosa glauca
○ ◌ VH ⋮ 1.5-2.2m · · 1.2-1.8m
A medium-sized shrub with attractive reddish violet, almost thornless stems, purple-blue leaves. Clear pink flowers in mid summer, followed by red hips in autumn. Prune in spring.

Taxus baccata Common yew
○ ◌ VH ⋮ 9-22m · · 7.5-9m
Evergreen conifer with dark green, flattened needles. Female plants bear fleshy, bright red fruit in winter. Also makes a good free-standing specimen.

Thuja plicata Western red cedar
○ ◌ VH ⋮ 20-30m · · 5-8m
Evergreen conifer. Ruddy brown bark peels with age. Dark green leaves have a pineapple aroma when crushed.

Specimen Trees and Shrubs

Arbutus unedo Strawberry tree
○ ◌ VH ⋮ 7.5m · · 7.5m
Evergreen tree. Attractive bark, glossy, deep green leaves. In autumn, clusters of white, urn-shaped, pendant flowers appear with red strawberry-like fruit.

Betula nigra Black birch
○ ❯ VH ⋮ 20m · · 10m
Deciduous, fast-growing tree. Pinky-orange, shaggy bark is brown and rigid on mature trees. Leaves diamond-shaped, fresh green, grey-green beneath.

Betula populifolia Grey birch
○ ◌ VH ⋮ 6-12m · · 5m
Creamy white bark. Catkins in early spring, followed by dark green leaves that turn pale yellow in autumn.

Betula utilis var. jacquemontii 'Silver Shadow' Himalayan birch
○ ◌ VH ⋮ 15m · · 7.5-9m
Deciduous, open-branched tree. White stems and large, drooping, dark green leaves turn butter yellow in autumn.

Cercis siliquastrum Judas tree
○ ◌ VH ⋮ 9m · · 9m
Clusters of bright pink, pea-like flowers in mid spring before heart-shaped leaves, followed by long, purple-red flat pods in summer.

Citrus aurantium Seville orange
○ ◌ <7 HH ⋮ 3-10m · · 5-8m
Widely branching evergreen with deep green leaves. Sweetly scented white flowers in spring followed by large, round, acidic, fruit.

Citrus limon Lemon
○ ◌ <7 TT ⋮ 3-10m · · 5-8m
Widely branching evergreen. Deep green, waxy, oval leaves, fragrant white flowers in spring followed by bitter yellow fruit.

Cordyline fruticosa Ti tree
○ ◌ Su TT ⋮ 2-4m · · 1-2m
Evergreen, upright shrub. Long, lance-shaped, green leaves. Many forms, with leaf colour ranging from purple-black through pink to yellow.

Cornus capitata
Bentham's cornel
○ ◌ <7 FH ⋮ 12m · · 12m
Semi-evergreen/evergreen spreading tree with oval, green-grey leaves. In spring, pale yellow bracts surround insignificant flowers, followed by large, strawberry-like red fruit.

Cornus florida
Flowering dogwood
○ ◌ <7 VH ⋮ 6-9m · · 6-9m
Deciduous tree with showy white bracts in late spring, followed by red fruit in autumn. Oval, pointed, dark green leaves turn purple in autumn.

Cotinus coggygria 'Notcutt's Variety' Smoke bush
○ ◌ VH ⋮ 3-4.5m · · 3-4.5m
Deciduous shrub with dark, purple-red foliage and smoky plumes of pink tinted flowers in spring.

Crinodendron hookerianum
Lantern tree
❯ ❯ <7 FH ⋮ 3m · · 7m
Evergreen, stiff-branched shrub with red, lantern-shaped pendulous flowers and dark green, narrow leaves. Requires a sheltered location with the plant base in cool shade.

Dacrydium cupressinum Rimu
○ ❯ FH ⋮ 10m · · 1.5m
Slow growing but very graceful, conical shaped conifer. Should be planted in a prominent position.

Euonymus fortunei 'Emerald 'n' Gold'
○ ◌ VH ⋮ 2m · · 3m
Evergreen, bushy, mound forming shrub. Bright green leaves, tinged pink in winter, have golden yellow margins. 'Silver Queen' has dark green leaves edged with white.

Ficus benghalensis Banyan
○ ❯ TT ⋮ 30m · · indefinite
Evergreen, spreading tree with tan coloured trunk and reddish brown aerial roots. Dark green, leathery leaves. Beautiful red figs in pairs.

Garrya elliptica Silk tassel bush
❯ ❯ VH ⋮ 6m · · 2.5-4m
Evergreen, bushy shrub with wavy edged, leathery, dark green leaves. In winter the whole plant is draped with grey-green catkins, longer on the male than on the female.

Gymnocladus dioica
Kentucky coffee tree
○ ◌ VH ⋮ 20m · · 15m
Deciduous tree grown for large leaves, pinkish when young, turning dark green in summer and yellow in autumn. Small, white star-shaped flowers in early summer.

Ilex verticillata Winterberry
○ ◌ VH ⋮ 2m · · 1.2-1.5m
Dense, suckering, deciduous shrub with oval, saw-toothed, bright green leaves. In autumn, female plants, if pollinated, bear a profusion of red berries that remain throughout the winter on the bare branches.

Juniperus communis 'Hibernica' Irish juniper
○ ◌ VH ⋮ 3-5m · · 30cm
Vigorous columnar conifer. Mid to yellow-green, glossy, aromatic leaves. Round fleshy fruit, used to flavour gin, are green at first, then blue-grey, ripening to black in third year.

Morus nigra Black mulberry
○ ◌ VH ⋮ 12m · · 15m
Round-headed, deciduous tree. Deep green, heart-shaped leaves turn yellow in autumn. Succulent, edible, purple-red fruit ripens in late summer. Tree becomes gnarled with age.

Myrtus communis
Common myrtle
○ ◌ FH ⋮ 3m · · 2.5-3m
Evergreen, dense, bushy shrub with oval, dark green, glossy aromatic leaves. Fragrant white flowers in mid spring followed by dark purple berries. Can be trimmed much like box.

Olea europaea Olive
○ ◌ FH ⋮ 10m · · 10m
Evergreen tree with oblong leaves, grey-green above, silvery beneath. Insignificant flowers, followed by edible green fruit that turns purple-black.

Pinus bungeana Lace-bark pine
○ ❯ VH ⋮ 10m · · 8m
Bushy, slow growing conifer with dark green leaves and smooth, grey-green bark flaking to reveal creamy yellow patches darkening to red or purple. Ornamental cones in autumn.

Pinus mugo Mountain pine
○ △ VH ⫶ 3-5m ·· 5-8m
Dense, bushy, spreading conifer with bright to dark green leaves and ornamental, medium-sized cones. The branches grow along the ground and then bend upwards. 'Ophir' is a dwarf cultivar with a compact bun-shape. The winter foliage is golden yellow.

Platanus orientalis
Oriental plane
○ △ VH ⫶ 25m ·· 25m
Deciduous, spreading tree producing large, glossy, pale-green palmate leaves and multicoloured, peeling bark. Inconspicuous flowers are followed by pendulous, spherical fruit clusters. Will tolerate polluted air.

Plumeria obtusa Frangipani
○ △ TT ⫶ 6m ·· 6m
Evergreen, open tree with long, very dark green, glossy leaves and clusters of fragrant, pure white flowers with a faint yellow centre.

Prunus x subhirtella
'Autumnalis' Higan cherry
○ △ VH ⫶ 8m ·· 8m
Deciduous spreading tree, bearing many small, white flowers tinged pink from late autumn to early spring. The leaves are oval and dark green, turning yellow in autumn.

Pseudowintera axillaris
Heropito
○ △ HH ⫶ 3-8m ·· 3-8m
Evergreen, rounded shrub with oval leaves, lustrous mid green above, grey-blue beneath. From late spring onwards, clusters of tiny, greenish-yellow flowers, followed by equally tiny, bright red globular fruit.

Quercus ilex Holm oak
○ △ >7 VH ⫶ 25m ·· 20m
Evergreen, dense, round-headed tree with dark, glossy green leaves, grey beneath. Small acorns in autumn. Can be wall trained.

Tabebuia aurea
Silver trumpet tree
○ △ TT ⫶ 7.5-10m ·· 5m
Slow growing evergreen with slender, irregular crown. Beautiful silvery grey-green, finger-like shaped leaves. Golden yellow flowers in clusters throughout the year.

Tamarix gallica Tamarisk
○ △ FH ⫶ 4m ·· 6m
Deciduous, spreading small tree with purple young shoots covered with tiny blue-grey leaves and sprays of pink flowers in summer.

Plants for Walls

Campsis radicans
Trumpet creeper
○ △ VH ⫶ 12m
Deciduous, woody-stemmed root climber with trumpet-shaped, orange-scarlet or yellow flowers in late summer and early autumn.

Chaenomeles japonica
Japanese quince
○ △ VH ⫶ 1m ·· 2m
Deciduous, thorny, spring-flowering shrub with bright red or red-orange flowers followed by yellow fruit. Can be untidy when free standing, but elegant when wall trained. *Chaenomeles speciosa* is slightly larger and bears clusters of bright red flowers from late winter until early spring.

Clematis armandii
○ △ FH ⫶ 3-5m ·· 2-3m
Evergreen, strong growing species with dark green, leathery leaves and fragrant white flowers in early spring. Requires a sheltered site on a sunny wall.

Clematis ligusticifolia
◗ △ VH ⫶ 6m ·· 3.5m
Deciduous, woody climber with slender stems, grey-green leaves, cup-shaped white flowers summer to autumn.

Clematis montana
○ △ VH ⫶ 7-12m ·· 2-3m
Deciduous clematis with masses of single white flowers in late spring. Best planted where it can rampage. 'Elizabeth' has pale pink, vanilla scented flowers.

Clematis 'Nellie Moser'
◗ △ FH ⫶ 3.5m ·· 1m
Rose-mauve flowers, carmine stripe on each petal, in early summer. Best planted on a shady wall to prevent flowers bleaching.

Cydonia oblonga Quince
○ △ VH ⫶ 5m ·· 5m
Deciduous tree with oval, dark green leaves. In spring, the whole tree is covered with large, pale pink flowers followed by fragrant, deep yellow fruit, often used for preserves.

Cytisus battandieri
Moroccan broom
○ △ VH ⫶ 6m ·· 4.5m
Semi-evergreen, open shrub with silver-green leaves. Grown for its racemes of pineapple-scented yellow flowers that appear from early to mid summer.

Ficus carica Common fig
○ △ >7 VH ⫶ 10m ·· 10m
Deciduous, multi-stemmed shrub with deeply lobed, light to dark green leaves. In hot climates edible fruit are produced in summer.

Fremontodendron californicum
Flannel bush
○ △ FH ⫶ 6m ·· 4m
Vigorous, semi-evergreen shrub with masses of large, showy, bright yellow, saucer-shaped flowers in summer amid dark green leaves. Best grown against a wall as habit can be untidy.

Hydrangea anomala subsp. petiolaris Climbing hydrangea
◗ △ VH ⫶ 9-15m
Deciduous, woody stemmed, self-clinging climber. In early summer, feathery clusters of tiny, cream-white flowers are produced on delicate stalks.

Jasminum officinale Jessamine
○ △ VH ⫶ 12m
Semi-evergreen, woody-stemmed, twinning climber. Grown for the deliciously scented clusters of small, white, star-shaped flowers that appear in summer and autumn. *J. o.* 'Aureum' has bright green leaves irregularly splashed with yellow.

Lapageria rosea
Chilean bellflower
◗ △ FH ⫶ 5m
Evergreen, woody-stemmed, twinning climber with oval, leathery, dark green leaves. Groups of waxy, rose-crimson, pendant, bell-shaped flowers from spring to autumn.

Lathyrus sylvestris
Narrow-leaved everlasting pea
○ △ VH ⫶ 2m
Herbaceous perennial with leaves comprising a pair of leaflets terminating in a tendril. Racemes of rose-pink flowers are borne in summer and early

autumn. Provide support and cut down in late autumn.

Magnolia grandiflora Bull bay
○ △ VH ⫶ 10m ·· 10m
Evergreen, rounded tree, often grown against a wall. Large, lemon-scented white flowers appear intermittently from spring to early autumn.

Malus domestica Apple
○ △ VH ⫶ 10m ·· 10m
Deciduous tree that can be wall trained into an espalier, cordon or fan. Attractive, scented, white or pink flowers in spring are followed by large, sweet fruit which ripens in autumn.

Mangifera indica Mango
○ △ TT ⫶ 25-28m ·· 30m
Dome-shaped, evergreen tree with large, pointed, glossy, deep green leaves. Pyramidal clusters of tiny, pinkish-white flowers in winter, followed by edible fruit.

Mespilus germanica Medlar
○ △ VH ⫶ 12m ·· 8m
Deciduous, spreading tree with white flowers in spring and summer followed in autumn by brown fruit, which is eaten when half rotten.

Parthenocissus henryana
◗ △ VH ⫶ 10m
Vigorous, deciduous, self-clinging climber. Leaves are green with white veins in summer, vivid red in autumn.

Parthenocissus tricuspidata
Boston ivy
◗ △ VH ⫶ 12-18m
Very vigorous, deciduous, self-clinging, woody-stemmed climber. Leaves lustrous green in summer, rich crimson to bright scarlet in autumn.

Passiflora vitifolia
Vine-leaved passion flower
○ △ TT ⫶ 6-10m
Vigorous climber with long, deep green leaves. Large, fragrant, vivid deep red flowers in summer, followed by small, velvety, supposedly edible fruit.

Plumbago indica
Indian leadwort
○ △ TT ⫶ 2m ·· 1-2m
Semi-evergreen/evergreen spreading shrub with mid green, oval leaves. Terminal racemes of red or pink primrose-shaped flowers in summer.

Prunus armeniaca Apricot
○ ◇ >7 VH ⫶ 8m ⟷ 8m
Deciduous, small, round headed tree.
White or pink tinged flowers in spring
followed by orangey, edible fruit.

Prunus avium Mazzard
○ ◇ >7 VH
⫶ 18-24m ⫶ 9-12m
Deciduous, spreading tree with red
banded bark. Sprays of white flowers
in spring followed by deep red fruit.
Leaves bronze at first, dark green in
summer, crimson in autumn.

Prunus cerasus Sour cherry
○ ◇ >7 VH ⫶ 5m ⟷ 6m
Deciduous, small, bushy tree. Dense
clusters of white flowers in late spring
followed by acid-tasting red or black
fruit. A parent of the Morello cherry.

Prunus domestica Plum
○ ◇ >7 VH ⫶ 5m ⟷ 6m
Deciduous, small, spineless tree with
pinky white flowers in spring followed
by purple, edible fruit.

Prunus dulcis Almond
○ ◇ VH ⫶ 8m ⟷ 8m
Deciduous, spreading tree bearing large
rose-pink to white flowers in late
winter and early spring.

Prunus persica Peach
○ ◇ >7 VH ⫶ 5m ⟷ 6m
Deciduous, small, bushy tree with
medium-sized pale pink flowers in early
spring followed by round, juicy fruit.

Punica granatum Pomegranate
○ ◇ HH ⫶ 2-8m ⟷ 2-8m
Deciduous, rounded tree with narrow,
oblong leaves. Bright red, funnel-
shaped flowers appear in summer
followed by spherical, edible fruit.

Pyrus communis Common pear
○ ◇ VH ⫶ 10m ⟷ 7m
Deciduous, narrowly conical tree.
White flowers appear with dark green
leaves in mid to late spring. Leaves turn
orange-red in the autumn.

Rosa 'Gloire de Dijon'
Old Glory Rose
○ ◇ VH ⫶ 4m ⟷ 2.5m
Vigorous, stiffly branched, climbing tea
or noisette rose. Large, fragrant, fully
double, quartered rosette, creamy-buff
flowers are borne from early summer
until the autumn.

Rosa 'Maigold'
○ ◇ VH ⫶ 2.5m ⟷ 2.5m
Vigorous, early flowering climbing
rose with prickly arched stems. Large,
fragrant, semi-double, cupped, bronze-
yellow flowers.

Stauntonia hexaphylla
○ ◇ FH ⫶ 10m
Evergreen, woody-stemmed, twinning
climber with dark green leaves. Small,
pale violet, fragrant, cup-shaped
flowers in spring.

Stephanotis floribunda
Madagascar jasmine
◗ ◇ TT ⫶ 5m
Evergreen climber with rope-like stems.
Clusters of small, waxy, pure white,
very fragrant flowers appear
periodically throughout the year.

Thunbergia erecta
Bush clock vine
◗ ◇ TT ⫶ 2-2.5m
Sprawling climber or untidy shrub
with funnel-shaped, violet-blue, yellow-
throated flowers throughout the year.

Trachelospermum asiaticum
○ ◇ HH ⫶ 6m
Evergreen, woody, much branched
twinning climber with masses of small,
very fragrant, white, cartwheel-shaped
flowers in summer.

Trachelospermum jasminoides
Star jasmine
○ ◇ HH ⫶ 9m
Woody-stemmed, twinning, evergreen
climber with clusters of very fragrant,
small, white flowers on the shoot ends
in summer. Glossy, lance-shaped leaves.

Tropaeolum speciosum
Flame creeper
○ ◇ VH ⫶ 4.5m
Rhizomatous, wiry, creeping
herbaceous, twinning climber with
blue-green leaves. Bright scarlet flowers
in summer followed by bright blue fruit
surrounded by deep red calyces.

Architectural Specimens

Acer palmatum var. dissectum
Japanese maple
◗ ◇ VH ⫶ 1.2m ⟷ 1.5m
Elegant, deciduous, low growing,
mound forming tree. Deeply divided,
feathery foliage is green in spring, then
turns a brilliant orange-red or yellow.
Best colour is achieved on acid soil.
A. p. var. dissectum 'Dissectum
Atropurpureum Group', bronze-red or
purple leaves turn scarlet in autumn.

Agave americana 'Variegata'
Variegated century plant
○ ◇ FH ⫶ 2m ⟷ 2m
Succulent perennial. Sword-shaped,
blue-green leaves edged yellow, from a
basal rosette. Tall flowering spike of
white flowers in spring and summer.

Agave parviflora
○ ◇ HH ⫶ 1.5m ⟷ 50cm
Succulent perennial with basal rosette
and upright, dark green leaves marked
white. Spike of white bell-shaped
flowers in summer.

Agave utahensis
○ ◇ HH ⫶ 23cm ⟷ 2m
Succulent perennial with basal rosette.
Upright, spiny, blue-grey leaves tippped
with long dark spine. Flower stem of
yellow flowers in summer.

Aloe vera Aloe
○ ◇ FH ⫶ 60cm ⟷ indefinite
A clump forming perennial with thick,
lance-like, mottled green leaves which
are toothed along the margins. The
metre-long flowering spikes carry bell-
shaped, deep yellow flowers in the
winter and spring.

Chamaerops humilis Dwarf
European fan palm
○ ◇ HH ⫶ 1.5m ⟷ 1.5m
Low growing evergreen palm with
elegant bright green to grey-green fan-
shaped leaves and erect flowering spike
of tiny yellow flowers in summer.

Chimonobambusa
quadrangularis
Square-stemmed bamboo
○ ◇ VH ⫶ 2.5-3m ⟷ indefinite
A creeping bamboo with beautiful dark
green, square canes, occasionally
splashed purple, and lance-shaped
leaves. The young shoots are edible.

Cordyline australis
'Torbay Dazzler' Cabbage tree
○ ◇ FH ⫶ 6-9m ⟷ 1.8-2.7m
Slow growing, evergreen tree usually
with a single stem topped with a dense
mass of sword-like leaves and large
plumes of creamy white, fragrant
flowers in early summer.

Cortaderia selloana
Pampas grass
○ ◇ VH ⫶ 2-3m ⟷ 1.2-1.5m
Evergreen, clump forming perennial
producing tussocks of grey-green,
arching leaves. Cream or silver plumes
on spikes 2-3m long in late summer.

Corylus avellana 'Contorta'
Corkscrew hazel
○ ◇ VH ⫶ 4.5-6m ⟷ 4.5-6m
Bushy deciduous shrub with bizarrely
twisted shoots and branches. Mid
green, broad, sharply-toothed leaves
have autumn colour. In late winter, bare
branches are hung with yellow catkins.

Cyathea cooperi Tree fern
◗ ◇ TT ⫶ to 12m ⟷ to 6m
A beautiful specimen for tropical
gardens. The trunk is crowned with
huge, light green, arching leaves divided
into small triangular-shaped leaflets.

Cynara cardunculus Cardoon
○ ◇ VH ⫶ 2.4m ⟷ 1-1.5m
Stately perennial with large clumps of
silver-grey, pointed lobed leaves that
arch gracefully. Massive stems carry
purple-blue, thistle-like flowerheads.

Dicksonia antarctica
Australian tree fern
◗ ◗ HH ⫶ 10m ⟷ 4m
Evergreen tree fern with stout trunk
covered in brown fibres and crowned
with large, arching, glossy to mid
green, finely divided fronds.

Dracaena marginata
Dragon tree
○ ◇ TT ⫶ 4.5m ⟷ 1-2m
Elegant, slow growing, erect tree with
much branched, slender trunk. Narrow,
strap-like leaves, green with red margin.

Echinopsis spachiana
Torch cactus
○ ◇ TT ⫶ 2m ⟷ 2m
Clump forming perennial with thick,
ribbed, glossy green stems and pale
gold spines along rib margins. White,
fragrant, funnel-shaped flowers open
on summer nights.

Echium vulgare Viper's bugloss
○ ◇ VH ⫶ 60-90cm ⟷ 30cm
Biennial with upright stems, narrow,
lance-shaped, dark green leaves. From
spring through summer, flowering spike
is covered with small, deep blue or
purplish trumpet-shaped flowers.

Echium wildpretii
Tower of Jewels

○ ◊ HH ⦂ 2.5m ·· 60cm

Erect, unbranched biennial. Rosette of narrow, lance-shaped silver leaves. In late spring and summer, compact spires bear small, red, funnel-shaped flowers.

Ensete ventricosum
Abyssinian banana

○ ◊ TT ⦂ 6m ·· 3m

Evergreen perennial. Short, stout trunk crowned with palm-like leaves, reddish mid rib. Flowers, intermittent, are reddish green with dark red bracts, followed by small, banana-like fruit.

Heliconia psittacorum
Parrot's flower

◗ ◊ TT ⦂ 2m ·· 1m

Tufted perennial with long-stalked, deep green, banana-like leaves. In summer, exotic-looking orange flowers with green tips and narrow red-orange glossy bracts.

Livistona chinensis
Chinese fan palm

○ ◊ TT ⦂ 12m ·· 7m

Slow growing, evergreen palm. Stout trunk, elegant, glossy, fan-shaped, arching leaves. In summer, mature trees bear insignificant flowers followed by loose clusters of black, berry-like fruit.

Mahonia japonica

◗ ◗ VH ⦂ 1.5-2.7m ·· 2.5-3.7m

Upright, evergreen shrub with deep glossy green leaves of many spiny leaflets that can turn red in direct sun. Long, spreading sprays of fragrant lemon-yellow flowers in winter, followed by blue-black berries.

Musa basjoo Japanese banana

○ ◊ VH ⦂ 3-5m ·· 2-2.5m

Suckering, evergreen, palm-like perennial with short trunk and broad, lance-like, bright green leaves up to 1m long. Pale yellow flowers in summer followed by inedible green fruit.

Opuntia robusta Prickly pear

○ ◊ TT ⦂ 5m ·· 5m

Bushy cactus with silvery blue, flattened, segmented spiny stems. Yellow saucer-shaped flowers in spring and summer.

Pachycereus marginatus
Organ-pipe cactus

○ ◊ TT ⦂ 7m ·· 3m

Perennial, columnar cactus. Ribbed,

shiny branching stem with minute spines along the rib edges. White funnel-shaped flowers in summer.

Pandanus pygmaeus
Dwarf screw-pine

○ ◊ TT ⦂ 1m ·· 60cm

Evergreen tree lacking a trunk. Narrow, beautifully marked leaves with horizontal yellow stripes.

Phormium 'Dazzler'
New Zealand flax

◗ ◊ VH ⦂ 1.8-3.7m ·· 1.2-1.8m

Evergreen, upright perennial with long, sword-shaped, stiff, dark green leaves vertically striped with red, bronze, salmon pink and yellow. Panicles of tubular, dull red flowers in summer. Good in coastal locations. *P. tenax* Purpureum Group has reddish purple to dark copper leaves, and reddish flowers. 'Sundowner' has bronzed green leaves with deep pink margins and pink flowers.

Phyllostachys nigra
Black bamboo

○ ◊ VH ⦂ 6-8m ·· indefinite

Clump forming bamboo with mid green leaves and arching canes, green at first, then mottled brown and black. *P. n.* var. *henonis* (Henon), canes bright green at first, later yellow-brown.

Pleioblastus variegatus
Dwarf white-striped bamboo

○ ◊ VH ⦂ 60-120cm

Evergreen species with pale green canes carrying spiky tufts of narrow, slightly downy, striped leaves. Spreads fairly quickly and can be invasive.

Pritchardia pacifica Fan palm

○ ◊ TT ⦂ 10m ·· 6m

Slow growing, graceful fan palm with ribbed, brown-ringed trunk and crown of arching, multi-segmented leaves.

Protea cynaroides King protea

○ ◊ <7 TT ⦂ 1.5m ·· 1.5m

Evergreen, rounded, bushy shrub with very large, spectacular, pink water lily-shaped flowerheads set in pink to red bracts, in spring and summer.

Selenicereus grandiflorus
Queen-of-the-night

◗ ◊ TT ⦂ 3m ·· indefinite

Spreading cactus with long, slender ribbed stems bearing clusters of short spines and supportive aerial roots. Large white flowers open at night in summer.

Trachycarpus fortunei
Chusan palm

○ ◊ VH ⦂ 9-15m ·· 2.5-3m

Evergreen palm with single trunk covered with fibers and crowned with large, arching, deeply divided mid green fronds. Sprays of cream-yellow, fragrant flowers in early summer.

Yucca gloriosa Spanish dagger

○ ◊ VH ⦂ 1.8-2.5m ·· 1.2-1.8m

Evergreen shrub. Stout stem crowned with rosettes of blue-green to dark green leaves. Panicles of bell-shaped flowers on flowering spike in summer.

Yucca whipplei
Our Lord's candle

○ ◊ HH ⦂ 1.5m ·· 90-120cm

Evergreen, almost stemless shrub. Forms a dense rosette of pointed, slender blue-green leaves. In late spring, the 3m flowering spike produces panicles of greenish-white, lemon-scented, bell-shaped flowers.

Overhead Cover

Bougainvillea spp.

○ ◊ TT ⦂ 7.5-12m ·· indefinite

A genus of spiny shrubs and vines with small oval leaves and small, tubular, short-lived flowers in clusters near the ends of the stems. The flowers are surrounded by brilliantly coloured, long lasting bracts. 'Barbara Karst' is a vining cultivar with brilliant, vivid purplish-red bracts; *B. glabra* 'Singapore Beauty', a large, dense vine with magenta bracts; *B. spectabilis*, a vigorous, large vine with rose to rose-reddish bracts.

Humulus lupulus Hop

○ ◊ VH ⦂ 6m

Herbaceous twinning climber with hairy stems and bristly, deeply lobed, light green toothed leaves. Greenish female flowerheads in pendant clusters in late summer.

Ipomoea tricolor 'Heavenly Blue'
Morning glory

○ ◊ TT ⦂ 3-4.5m

Short-lived, twinning perennial climber with soft, hairy stems, best grown as an annual. In summer, white throated, deep purple to blue-purple funnel-shaped flowers.

Lonicera periclymenum
Honeysuckle

○ ◊ VH ⦂ 7m

Deciduous, woody-stemmed twinning climber with oval leaves and fragrant, tubular, white and yellow flowers flushed pink and red, in spring and summer. 'Graham Thomas' has flowers that are white in bud, opening yellow.

Vitis coignetiae
Crimson glory vine

◗ ◊ VH ⦂ 15m

Vigorous, deciduous, woody-stemmed, tendril climber with large, heart-shaped leaves, dark green turning orange-purple-brown and scarlet in autumn. Tiny, pale green flowers followed by inedible black berries.

Vitis vinifera Grape vine

○ ◊ VH ⦂ 9m

Leathery, dark green, lobed leaf broadly rounded in outline, turns red in autumn. Tiny, pale green flowers in summer are followed by edible fruit.

Wisteria floribunda
Japanese wisteria

○ ◊ VH ⦂ 9m

Deciduous, twinning, woody-stemmed climber with light to mid green leaves of oval leaflets that appear with drooping racemes of fragrant, violet-blue, pea-like flowers in early summer. 'Alba' has white flowers.

Wisteria frutescens
American wisteria

○ ◊ VH ⦂ 9m

Deciduous, twinning, woody-stemmed climber with leaves of ovate leaflets. Racemes of fragrant flowers, pale lilac-purple with a yellow spot, in summer.

Wisteria sinensis
Chinese wisteria

○ ◊ VH ⦂ 30m

Vigorous, deciduous, twinning, woody-stemmed climber. Racemes of fragrant mauve-lilac or pale violet flowers in early summer, followed by velvety pods. 'Alba' is a white cultivar.

Foliage Plants

Acalypha wilkesiana
'Godseffiana' Copper leaf plant

○ ▶ TT ⵗ 5 m ·· 4m

Woody shrub with large, concave, bronze-green leaves daubed red, purple and copper, almost as wide as long. Narrow, tail-like spikes of red flowers are borne intermittently.

Acanthus spinosus
Bear's breeches

○ △ VH ⵗ 1.2m ·· 60cm

Herbaceous perennial with large, deeply cut, arching leaves with sharp spines. Spires of mauve-and-white, funnel-shaped flowers in summer. Protect crowns in the first winter after planting.

Adiantum pedatum
Northern maidenhair fern

▶ ▶ <7 VH ⵗ 45cm ·· 45cm

Vigorous, semi-evergreen fern. Upright, slightly arching mid green, finger-like, divided fronds are slightly wavy. Remove fading fronds regularly.

Adiantum venustum
Maidenhair fern

▶ ▶ <7 HH ⵗ 23cm ·· 30cm

Deciduous fern with pale green, delicate fronds tinged brown when young. Glossy stems bear many triangular leaflets that give a delicate, arching appearance. Best on acid soil.

Aechmea fosteriana Living vase

○ △ TT ⵗ 60cm ·· 30cm

A bromeliad with a dramatically coloured tubular vase of stiff, erect, light green leaves, banded purple-brown beneath. Flowering spike of red bracts and yellow flowers.

Alocasia sanderiana
Elephant ear

▶ △ TT ⵗ 1m ·· 60cm

Evergreen, clump forming perennial grown for its striking, heart-shaped, wavy-edged, dark green leaves with white veins. Insignificant flower spike in summer.

Asplenium scolopendrium
Hart's-tongue fern

▶ ▶ VH ⵗ 30-60cm ·· 25-50cm

Evergreen/semi-evergreen with tufts of light green, upright, lance-shaped leathery fronds. Suitable for limey soils.

Asplenium trichomanes
Maidenhair spleenwort

▶ ▶ VH ⵗ 15cm ·· 15-30cm

Semi-evergreen fern with long, slender, tapering fronds of dark green leaflets with rounded tips. Thin stems are dark glossy brown to black.

Athyrium filix-femina
Lady fern

▶ ▶ VH ⵗ 45-90cm ·· 45-90cm

Dainty, much divided, pale green, arching, lance-shaped fronds arising from erect rhizomes and divided into long, pointed leaflets.

Bergenia ciliata Elephant's ears

○ △ VH ⵗ 30-35cm ·· 50cm

Clump forming, semi-evergreen perennial with large, rounded, hairy leaves. In spring, clusters of white flowers that turn pink with age.

Blechnum chilense
Chilean hard fern

▶ ▶ FH ⵗ 30cm-1m ·· 30-60cm

Evergreen/semi-evergreen fern with a ring of lance-shaped, mid green outer fronds heavily indented and arranged symmetrically, inside which is an inner ring of fringed, brown fronds.

Codiaeum variegatum
var. pictum Croton

○ ○ TT ⵗ 1.3m ·· 1.3m

Evergreen, sparingly-branched, erect shrub with exotic, glossy, leathery leaves varying in shape and size. Colouring also varies, the variegation a mix of yellow, pink, orange or red.

Dryopteris filix-mas Male fern

● ▶ VH ⵗ 1.2m ·· 1m

Semi-evergreen/deciduous fern with spear-shaped, finely divided, deep glossy green arching fronds arranged in a shuttlecock shape.

Festuca glauca Blue fescue

○ △ VH ⵗ 15-30cm ·· 20-25cm

Tufty, evergreen perennial grass. Narrow leaves in shades from blue-green to silvery white, forming a domed mound. Stiff, upright stems with violet tinged flowering plumes in summer.

Gunnera tinctoria

○ ▶ VH ⵗ 1.5m ·· 1.5m

Perennial with large, rounded, puckered and lobed leaves. Tiny, reddish green flowers in early summer.

Hakonechloa macra 'Aureola'

○ △ VH ⵗ 40cm ·· 45-60cm

Slow growing perennial grass. Purple stems, tapering, ribbon-like, arching leaves. Young leaves bright yellow, finely striped green, often ageing to reddish brown.

Helictotrichon sempervirens
Blue oat grass

○ △ VH ⵗ 90-120cm ·· 60cm

Evergreen perennial with stiff, narrow, silver-blue leaves. Straw-coloured flowering spikes appear in summer.

Hosta species and cultivars
Funkia

▶ △ VH

ⵗ & ·· *See individual species*

Genus of clump forming perennials grown primarily for their decorative foliage, useful as ground cover in shade, but slug damage is a problem. Flowering spikes are held well above the foliage in summer.

H. crispula ⵗ 75cm ·· 1m
Large oval to heart-shaped, wavy edged leaves, dark green with irregular margins. Pale mauve, trumpet-shaped flowers.

H. fortunei var. *aureomarginata*
ⵗ 75cm-1m ·· 1m
Oval to heart-shaped, mid green leaves with an irregular, creamy yellow edge. Violet trumpet-shaped flowers. Will tolerate full sun.

H. 'Halcyon' ⵗ 30cm ·· 1m
Heart-shaped, blue-grey leaves. Cluster of trumpet-shaped, violet-mauve flowers.

H. sieboldiana ⵗ 1m ·· 1.5m
Large, blue-grey, heart-shaped leaves, puckered and deeply ribbed. Very pale lilac, trumpet-shaped flowers.

H. sieboldii ⵗ 45cm ·· 60cm
Vigorous. Mid to dark green, lance-shaped, round tipped leaves with white edges. Violet, trumpet- shaped flowers.

H. ventricosa ⵗ 70cm ·· 1m
Glossy, dark green, heart-shaped leaves with slightly wavy edges. Deep purple bell-shaped flowers.

Myosotidium hortensia
Chatham Island forget-me-not

▶ ▶ FH ⵗ 45-60cm ·· 60cm

Evergreen perennial. Large, glossy, ribbed, sometimes curled leaves. Large globes of blue forget-me-not flowers in summer. Resents being moved.

Neoregelia carolinae
Blushing bromeliad

▶ △ TT ⵗ 20-30cm ·· 40-60cm

Evergreen. Bright green, lustrous, strap-shaped, finely toothed, spiny leaves. In summer, clusters of compact. tubular blue-purple flowers with red bracts.

Onopordum acanthium
Cotton thistle

○ △ VH ⵗ 1.8m ·· 90cm

Branching, slow growing, erect biennial. Large, lobed, spiny, bright silver-grey leaves. Deep purple flowerheads in summer.

Polystichum setiferum
Soft shield fern

▶ ▶ VH ⵗ 60-120cm ·· 75-90cm

Semi-evergreen/evergreen with broadly lance-shaped, divided, soft textured, dark green fronds.

Smyrnium olusatrum
Alexanders

○ △ VH ⵗ 60-150cm ·· 1m

Slow growing, upright biennial with shiny, bright green leaves. In late spring clusters of large, yellow-green flowers followed by smooth, black fruit.

Ground Cover

Ajuga reptans Bugle

○ ▶ VH ⵗ 15cm ·· 1m

Evergreen creeping perennial. Short spikes of bright blue flowers in spring. Spoon-shaped leaves are dark green. Will tolerate both sun and shade.

Alchemilla mollis Lady's mantle

▶ △ VH ⵗ 50cm ·· 50cm

Perennial. Rounded, pale green leaves, crinkled edges. Sprays of tiny green-yellow flowers in mid summer.

Asarum canadense
Canadian wild ginger

▶ △ VH ⵗ 10cm ·· 15cm

Low growing perennial with leathery, dark green, oval leaves. Small brown-purple flowers with unpleasant smell in spring.

Convolvulus sabatius
Moroccan convolvulus

○ △ VH ↕ 15-20cm ↔ 30cm

Trailing perennial with narrow stems covered with small, oval leaves. In summer and early autumn, vibrant, blue-purple trumpet-shaped flowers.

Dorotheanthus bellidiformis
Livingstone daisy

○ △ TT ↕ 15cm ↔ 30cm

Annual. Carpet of fleshy, lance-shaped grey-green to green leaves. Dazzling, small daisy-like flowers in shades of red, orange, yellow and pink.

Hedera helix Common ivy

◗ △ VH ↕ 10m ↔ 5m

Self-clinging or trailing evergreen perennial. Dark green, glossy, lobed leaves with paler veins. Insignificant, pale green flowers in summer followed by black berries. May become invasive.

Hosta species

All species of *Hosta* can be used as effective ground cover. See Foliage Plants (page 149) for details.

Hypoestes phyllostachya
Polka-dot plant

○ △ TT ↕ 75cm ↔ 75cm

Evergreen perennial with deep green, heart-shaped leaves flecked with pink or purplish spots. Small, lavender, tubular-shaped flowers intermittently throughout the year.

Impatiens hawkeri
New Guinea impatiens

◗ △ TT ↕ 60cm ↔ 30cm

Herbaceous perennial usually grown as an annual. Reddish, succulent stems. Serrated, ovate leaves, red mid rib. Large flowers are brilliant red. *I. platypetala* has shorter leaves and smaller, carmine red flowers.

Lamium galeobdolon
Yellow archangel

○ △ VH ↕ 30cm ↔ indefinite

Semi-evergreen perennial. Oval, mid green leaves marked silver. Small, yellow, hooded flowers in late spring.

Mahonia aquifolium
Oregon grape

◗ ◗ VH ↕ 60-90cm ↔ 90-150cm

Evergreen shrub. Forms a dense thicket. Glossy green, oval leaflets often red or purple in winter Yellow flowers in spring followed by blue-black berries.

Pereskia aculeata
Barbados gooseberry

○ △ TT ↕ 10m ↔ 5m

Deciduous, spreading cactus with spiny stems. Thick, fleshy leaves, dark green with black spines. Large, fragrant, white, yellow or pinkish flowers with orange centres throughout summer.

Phlox divaricata Blue phlox

◗ △ VH ↕ 30cm ↔ 20cm

Semi-evergreen, spreading perennial. Oval leaves. In early summer, clusters of lavender-blue, saucer-shaped flowers.

Pulmonaria officinalis
Lungwort

○ △ VH ↕ 25-30cm ↔ 30-45cm

Spreading, evergreen perennial. Bristly, heart-shaped, silver spotted leaves. Pink flowers, early to late spring, age to violet and blue. Shade tolerant.

Rubus tricolor

○ △ FH ↕ 60cm ↔ 2m

Evergreen shrub. Prostrate and arching shoots with soft red bristles. Dark green, glossy, oval, toothed leaves and white cup-shaped flowers in mid summer. Edible black fruit.

Saxifraga cuneifolia
Lesser London pride

◗ ◗ VH ↕ 15-20cm ↔ 30cm

Evergreen perennial. Carpet of rounded-leaf rosettes, late spring to early summer. Panicles of tiny, white flowers with red, pink or yellow spots.

Saxifraga sempervivum
Saxifrage

◗ △ VH ↕ 10-15cm ↔ 10-15cm

Hummock forming, evergreen perennial. Tufted silver-green leaves in tight rosettes. Racemes of deep red flowers in early spring.

Tradescantia spathacea
Moses-in-a-Boat

○ △ TT ↕ 45cm ↔ 45cm

Clump forming perennial. Lance-shaped, stiff, succulent leaves on very short stems, deep green above, deep purple-red below. Small white flowers are inside two large, purple, boat-shaped bracts.

Tradescantia virginiana
Spiderwort

○ △ VH ↕ 35cm ↔ 60cm

Clump forming perennial with strap-shaped green leaves tumbling over one another. From spring to early summer,

clusters of triangular-shaped, blue, pink or white flowers.

Tropaeolum majus Nasturtium

○ △ TT ↕ 30cm ↔ 1m

Fast growing, trailing annual. Bright green, round leaves. Trumpet-shaped flowers in all shades of red and yellow, from summer until autumn. Edible flowers and leaves.

Vinca minor Lesser periwinkle

◗ ◗ VH ↕ 30cm ↔ 1.5m

Prostrate, spreading, mat forming evergreen sub-shrub. Stems covered with small, glossy, dark green oval leaves. Small, purple-blue flowers, mid spring to early summer

Herbs

Achillea millefolium Yarrow

○ △ VH ↕ 80cm ↔ 60cm

Vigorous, upright perennial with fern-like foliage and small white flowers on large plate-like flowerheads in summer. Can be dried for winter decoration.

Allium sativum Garlic

○ △ VH ↕ 60cm ↔ 22cm

Grown as a culinary crop for its corms or cloves. Thin, lance-shaped, erect leaves. Often the flowerhead never opens beyond the bud stage, but tiny bulbs form between the flower buds.

Allium schoenoprasum Chives

○ △ VH ↕ 30 cm ↔ 5-10cm

Hardy, clump forming bulb with narrow, aromatic, hollow, erect, dark green leaves. In summer, globes of tiny bell-shaped, purple flowers.

Anethum graveolens Dill

○ △ VH ↕ 60-150cm ↔ 30cm

Upright annual with branching, fine, feathery, aromatic leaves. Flattened flowerheads of tiny, yellow-green flowers in summer.

Artemisia abrotanum
Lad's love/Southernwood

○ △ VH ↕ 75cm ↔ 75cm

Semi-evergreen/deciduous bushy shrub with grey-green to silver-grey, aromatic leaves. Clusters of insignificant yellow flowers in late summer.

Artemisia absinthium
Wormwood

○ △ VH ↕ 1m ↔ 1.2m

Woody, evergreen, bushy perennial with finely divided, grey-green, aromatic leaves. In summer, tiny, insignificant grey flowerheads on long sprays. Not to be ingested.

Chamaemelum nobile
Chamomile

○ △ VH ↕ 10cm ↔ 45cm

Evergreen, mat forming perennial. Short, aromatic, finely divided, bright green leaves. White daisy-like flowers with yellow centres in late summer.

Coriandrum sativum Coriander

○ △ VH ↕ 60cm ↔ 30cm

Tender, upright annual with white flowers in summer, grown for the aromatic, bright green leaves and seeds.

Foeniculum vulgare Fennel

○ △ VH ↕ 2m ↔ 45cm

Erect, branching perennial with finely divided, feathery, bright green leaves. Large, flat plates of small yellow flowers in summer. All parts of the plant are used for culinary purposes.

Hyssopus officinalis Hyssop

○ △ Su VH ↕ 60cm ↔ 1m

Semi-evergreen/deciduous, upright, dense shrub. Bright green, narrow aromatic leaves. Dense clusters of dark blue flowers from mid summer to early autumn. Can be clipped for edging.

Laurus nobilis Bay laurel

○ △ VH ↕ 3-10m ↔ 2.5-5m

Untidy shrub that can be trimmed and shaped. Glossy, dark green, narrowly oval, very aromatic leaves. In spring, small, pale, star-shaped flowers followed by black fruit.

Lavandula angustifolia
Lavender

○ △ VH ↕ 30-90cm ↔ 30-120cm

Evergreen, bushy shrub with narrow, aromatic, silver-grey leaves. Spikes of very fragrant, mauve-purple flowers in summer. *L. a.* 'Alba' has white flowers.

Lavandula stoechas
French lavender

○ △ VH ↕ 50-75cm ↔ 50-75cm

Bushy, dense, evergreen shrub with narrow, silver-grey, aromatic leaves. In summer, flowering spikes of tiny, fragrant, deep purple flowers are capped with a feathery, showy bract.

Mentha spicata Spearmint

○ △ VH | 45-60cm ·· indefinite

Hardy perennial. Aromatic, dark green serrated leaves, purple-mauve flowers in the summer.

Mentha x *piperita* Peppermint

○ △ VH | 30-60cm ·· indefinite

Hardy perennial. Aromatic, oval, slightly toothed, mid green leaves. Reddish green stems bear spikes of small purple flowers in summer.

Monarda citriodora 'Croftway Pink' Bergamot

▶ △ VH | 1m ·· 45cm

Clump forming perennial with whorls of soft pink flowers in summer above aromatic, oval, toothed, mid green, hairy leaves.

Nepeta nervosa Catmint

○ △ VH | 35cm ·· 30cm

Clump forming perennial. Arching stems with pointed, lance-shaped, mid green leaves. Small, pale-blue, tubular flowers from early to mid summer.

Nepeta x *faassenii* Catmint

○ △ VH | 45-60cm ·· 45-60cm

Bushy, clump forming perennial. Makes a good edging plant. Forms mounds of small, greyish-green leaves with loose spikes of soft, lavender-blue, tubular flowers in early summer.

Ocimum basilicum Basil

○ △ TT | 45cm ·· 10cm

Tender, upright annual. Strongly aromatic, bright green, oval leaves that are widely used in Mediterranean cookery and salads. Do not allow to flower if using for cookery.

Origanum dictamnus Dittany of Crete

○ △ VH | 12-15cm ·· 40cm

Spreading herbaceous perennial with a prostrate habit. Small, aromatic, white felted leaves and tiny flowers set within purplish bracts. Perfect for the rock garden; tea made from the leaves is considered a panacea.

Origanum majorana Marjoram

○ △ FH | 30cm ·· 30cm

Sub-shrub often grown as an annual. Highly aromatic, round, pale-green leaves. Tiny white flowers in summer.

Origanum vulgare Oregano

○ △ VH | 45cm ·· 45cm

Spreading, mat forming perennial. Dark green, aromatic leaves, slightly hairy. Clusters of tiny, tubular, mauve flowers in summer. *O. v.* ssp. *hirtum* (Greek oregano), hairy, grey-green leaves, tubular white flowers.

Osmorhiza longistylis Anise root

○ △ Su VH

| 45-90 cm ·· 45-90 cm

Deciduous perennial. Inconspicuous white flowers in loose, flat, plate-like heads. Oval leaves in groups of 3.

Petroselinum crispum Parsley

○ △ VH | 30-40cm ·· 30cm

Hardy biennial. Bright green, curly, mildly flavoured leaves. Flat plates of small, cream-white flowers in summer.

Phlomis fruticosa Jerusalem sage

○ △ FH | 1.2m ·· 1.2m

Spreading, evergreen shrub with upright shoots. Lance-shaped, sage-like, grey-green, silver-edged leaves. Deep yellow-gold flowers in summer.

Rosmarinus officinalis Rosemary

○ △ VH | 1.5-1.8m ·· 1.5m

Dense, bushy, evergreen shrub. Aromatic, narrow, grey-green, needle-like leaves, silver beneath. Small, purplish-blue flowers from mid spring to early summer.

Ruta graveolens Common rue

○ △ VH | 60-90cm ·· 60-75cm

Bushy, compact, evergreen sub-shrub. Pungent, finely-divided, blue-green leaves, greenish-yellow flowers in summer. Can cause skin rash.

Santolina chamaecyparissus Cotton lavender

○ △ VH | 75cm ·· 1m

Evergreen, dense, rounded shrub. Narrowly oblong, white leaves on grey-white, felted stems. From mid to late summer, bright yellow button flowers.

Stachys officinalis Betony

○ △ VH | 45-60cm ·· 30-45cm

Mat forming perennial with oval, mid green, round-toothed leaves. In summer, clusters of pink, purple or white tubular flowers on sturdy stems. Not for ingestion.

Symphytum officinale Comfrey

○ △ VH | 1m ·· 1m

Vigorous, coarse, upright perennial with lance-shaped, hairy, rich green leaves. Creamy yellow or purplish flowers on hairy stems, in summer.

Tanacetum cinerariifolium Pyrethrum

○ △ FH | 30-37cm ·· 20cm

Hardy perennial. Finely divided, grey-green leaves, white beneath. Long flowering stalks crowned with daisy-like flowers, white with a yellow centre, in summer.

Tanacetum parthenium Feverfew

○ △ VH | 20-45cm ·· 20-45cm

Moderately fast growing, short-lived, bushy perennial often grown as an annual. Aromatic, lobed, mid green leaves. Small, daisy-like, yellow-centred white flowerheads in summer.

Tanacetum vulgare Tansy

○ △ VH | 90cm ·· 30-60cm

Hardy perennial. Aromatic, deeply indented, dark green, toothed leaves. Yellow button-like flowers in late summer. Do not ingest.

Thymus vulgaris Garden thyme

○ △ VH | 15-30cm ·· 40cm

Bushy, mat forming, hardy, evergreen perennial. Thin, deep green, aromatic leaves, mauve flowers in summer.

Verbena officinalis Vervain

○ △ VH | 60-90cm ·· 30cm

Upright, hardy perennial. Bright green, hairy, deeply divided leaves. Small, pale lilac flowers in summer. Avoid during pregnancy.

Container Plants

Agapanthus 'Albatross' African Lily

○ ▶ Su FH | 1m ·· 20in

Clump forming, evergreen perennial. Large dense globes of white flowers on strong stems in late summer. Strap-shaped, broad, dark green leaves. Headbourne Hybrids have white, deep or pale blue flowers in summer.

Amaryllis belladonna Belladonna lily

○ △ FH | 50-80cm ·· 30-45cm

Autumn flowering bulb. Large, bright pink, trumpet-shaped flowers on a purple stem. Strap-shaped leaves appear after flowering.

Bracteantha bracteata Everlasting flower

○ △ FH | 30-120cm ·· 20-30cm

Perennial commonly grown as an annual. Papery, daisy-like flowerheads, yellow, orange, red to pink and white, in summer. Ideal for dried flowers.

Camellia saluenensis Camellia

▶ △ VH | 4m ·· 2.5m

Fast growing, evergreen shrub with lance-shaped, dark green leaves. White to rose red flowers in early spring.

Canna indica Canna lily

○ ▶ VH | 1.2m ·· 45-60cm

Showy, rhizomatous perennial. Large, deep green, veined, paddle-like leaves. In summer, bold spike of large, orchid-like, bright red flowers.

Cistus ladanifer Rock rose

○ △ VH | 1.5-1.8m ·· 1.2-1.5m

Leggy, upright, evergreen shrub. Dark green, narrow, aromatic, sticky leaves. Large, white, cup-shaped flowers with central red markings, in early summer.

Crocus biflorus Crocus

○ △ VH | 10cm ·· 2.5-8cm

Early spring corm. Upright, white-purple flowers, yellow throats, purple striped outside. Narrow basal leaves, each with a white stripe.

Cyclamen hederifolium Cyclamen

▶ △ VH | 10cm ·· 15-25cm

Autumn flowering tuber. Pale to deep pink flowers, heart-shaped, ivy-like leaves patterned in silvery green.

Dianthus caryophyllus Carnation

○ △ VH | 80 cm ·· 45 cm

Loosely tufted, upright perennial with narrow, silver-grey leaves. Clusters of very fragrant, bright pink-purple flowers in summer

Epimedium perralderianum Barrenwort

▶ △ VH | 25-35cm ·· 45-60cm

Evergreen perennial. Large leaves of 3 toothed leaflets, bronzy when young, later glossy green. In spring, clusters of small, pendent, bright yellow flowers.

Eryngium bourgatii Sea holly
○ △ VH ⁝ 30-60cm · · 30-45cm
Clump forming perennial with curved, prickly, jagged leaves, veined and spangled with silver. Branched, blue stems crowned with thistle-like, blue-green, then lilac-blue flowers are borne from mid to late summer.

Erythronium americanum
Yellow adder's tongue
◗ △ Sp VH ⁝ 5-25cm · · 5-8cm
Spring flowering tuber with pendent yellow flowers, bronze tinted on the outside, bright yellow inside, appear on brown stalks above a pair of semi-erect, mottled green-and-brown basal leaves.

Erythronium californicum
Californian fawn lily
◗ △ Sp VH ⁝ 15-45cm · · 10-15cm
Spring flowering tuber. Above the heavily mottled, dark green, glossy leaves, appear flowering stalks bearing white or cream-white flowers with orange-brown marks, recurved petals.

Erythronium dens-canis
Dog's-tooth violet
◗ △ Sp VH ⁝ 10-15cm · · 10cm
Spring flowering tuber. Mottled green, spear-shaped leaves, above which the flowering stems bears nodding flowers with recurved petals that are pink-purple or white and usually banded brown near the centre.

Fritillaria imperialis
Crown imperial
○ △ VH ⁝ 60-120cm · · 20-30cm
Spring flowering bulb of stately grandeur. The stout stem is surrounded by clusters of twisted, glossy leaves, crowned by a ring of pendulous, bell-shaped, orange flowers capped by a tuft of leaves.

Hamamelis virginiana
Virginian witch hazel
○ △ <7 VH ⁝ 4m · · 4m
Deciduous, upright, open small tree. Small, fragrant, spidery yellow flowers appear on the bare branches in winter. The broadly oval leaves turn yellow in the autumn.

Hedychium gardnerianum
Kahili ginger
○ ◗ HH ⁝ 1.5-2m · · 75cm
Upright, rhizomatous perennial with lance-shaped, grey-green leaves. From late summer to early autumn, the flowering spike bears many delicate, butterfly-like, fragrant, lemon-yellow and red flowers.

Hemerocallis citrina Day lily
○ ◗ VH ⁝ 75cm · · 75cm
Vigorous, clump forming perennial with dark green, strap-shaped leaves. Very fragrant, rich lemon-yellow, trumpet-shaped flowers in succession throughout mid summer.

Hibiscus schizopetalus
Japanese hibiscus
○ ◌ TT ⁝ 3m · · 2m
Large, evergreen shrub with graceful drooping branches and small, heart-shaped, deep green leaves. Pendent, scarlet to pink blossoms on a long stalk. Can be trained as a climber.

Hosta undulata var. albomarginata Funkia
◗ ◌ VH ⁝ 50-60cm · · 50-60cm
Graceful perennial. Dark green, heart-shaped, smooth leaves with irregular white margin, which barely reaches the pointed tip. Bell-shaped, mauve flowers appear on a tall stalk in early summer.

Iris germanica
Common German flag iris
○ ◌ VH ⁝ 60-120cm · · indefinite
Rhizomatous bearded iris. Arching, sword-like leaves. In late spring and early summer, yellow flowers, bearded blue-purple to violet.

Isoplexis canariensis
○ △ TT ⁝ 1.5m · · 75cm
Evergreen, sparsely branched rounded shrub. In summer, beautiful foxglove-like red to orange-brown flowers on dense, upright, spikes. Strap-like leaves.

Kniphofia caulescens
Red-hot poker
○ △ VH ⁝ 1.2m · · 60cm
Evergreen, upright perennial. Tuft of arching, narrow, lance-shaped, blue-green leaves. Stout stems bear terminal flower spikes of small, tubular reddish pink flowers in autumn.

Lilium martagon Martagon lily
○ △ VH ⁝ 1-1.5m · · 15-25cm
Summer flowering bulb. Lance-shaped, oval leaves, scented, turkscap flowers in pink or purple with darker spots.

Linaria purpurea
Purple toadflax
○ △ VH ⁝ 75-90cm · · 30-45cm
Upright perennial with narrow, oval, grey-green leaves. In mid to late summer, racemes of tiny, snapdragon-like, purple-blue flowers, with touches of white at the throat.

Magnolia stellata Star magnolia
○ △ VH ⁝ 2.5-3m · · 2.5-3.7m
Deciduous, dense, bushy shrub with grey-green flower buds tht burst open in early spring to reveal fragrant, white, star-shaped flowers. Narrow, deep green leaves.

Narcissus poeticus
Pheasant's eye narcissus
○ △ VH ⁝ 22-42cm · · 7.5-10cm
Late spring flowering bulb with fragrant flowers comprising small, shallow, yellow to orange cup with a red rim and glistening white collar. Narrow, erect, grey-green leaves.

Neoregelia ampullaceae
Bromeliad
◗ ◗ TT ⁝ 15cm · · 15cm
Beautiful small, elegant bromeliad with light green, strap-like leaves spotted reddish brown. Lovely violet flowers complement the green leaves.

Nerium oleander 'Hawaii'
Oleander
○ △ FH ⁝ 2m · · 2m
Drought tolerant, upright, dwarf bush/evergreen shrub with leathery, dark green leaves. Flaring funnel-shaped, deep salmon-pink flowers from spring to autumn.

Nicotiana alata
Flowering tobacco
○ △ FH ⁝ 75cm · · 30cm
Rosette forming perennial commonly grown as an annual. Clusters of tubular, cream-white flowers in late summer, very fragrant in the evening. The leaves are oval and mid green.

Ophiopogon planiscapus 'Nigrescens' Black mondo grass
○ △ VH ⁝ 15-30cm · · 30cm
Evergreen, clump forming, spreading perennial. Narrow, upright, almost black, grass-like leaves. Racemes of small, mauve flowers in summer are followed by small, shiny black berries.

Pelargonium 'Voodoo'
Geranium
○ △ TT ⁝ 60cm · · 25cm
Evergreen, upright, fleshy perennial, more correctly known as a zonal pelargonium. Large, wine red flowers with dark purple centres in summer. Round, lobed, dark green leaves.

Phormium tenax Purpureum Group New Zealand flax
◗ △ VH ⁝ 1.8-3.7m · · 1.2-1.8m
Evergreen, upright perennial with long, sword-shaped, stiff reddish-purple to dark copper leaves. Short, purple-blue flowering spike produces panicles of tubular, reddish flowers in summer.

Rhododendron yakushimanum
◗ △ VH ⁝ 1m · · 1.5m
Neat, compact, dome-shaped evergreen. Oval leaves, brown felted beneath, silvery at first, mature to deep green. Funnel-shaped pink flowers, green-flecked within, fade to white in late spring. R.y. 'Bambi', red buds open to pale pink flowers flushed yellow. R.y. 'Koichiro Wada', rose pink flower buds open to clear white flowers.

Romneya coulteri
Californian tree poppy
○ △ VH ⁝ 1.2-2.5m · · 1.2-2.5m
Bushy, vigorous summer flowering sub-shrub. Large, fragrant, papery white flowers with prominent yellow centres. Grey leaves, deeply divided.

Rosa 'Coral Dawn'
○ △ VH ⁝ 3.5m · · 2m
Modern climbing rose with dark green leaflets. Clumps of coral-pink, semi-double flowers in summer; repeats in autumn. Will tolerate a shady wall.

Rosa gallica 'Versicolor'
Rosa Mundi
○ △ VH ⁝ 75cm · · 1m
Old, well loved rose, neat and bushy. Semi-double, slightly scented, flat flowers, rose-red striped with white, are borne in the summer.

Rosa 'Indigo'
○ △ VH ⁝ 1.2m · · 60cm
An old fashioned rose with an upright habit bearing richly scented, vicious purple, goblet-shaped flowers on long flowering stems. The foliage is dark green, tinged dark red.

Sanseviria trifasciata
Mother-in-law's tongue
○ △ TT ⁝ 1-1.2m · · 10cm
Tender perennial. Rosette of erect, fleshy, pointed stiff leaves, light silver-green with jagged, deep green horizontal bands.

Strelitzia reginae
Bird of paradise

○ △ TT ↧ 1-1.2m ·· 75cm
Evergreen, clump forming perennial. Long, grey-green, paddle-like leaves. Exotic, beak-like, orange and blue flowers surrounded by red-edged, boat-shaped bracts, mainly in spring.

Taxus baccata 'Fastigiata'
Irish yew

○ △ VH ↧ 10-15m ·· 4-5m
Evergreen conifer. E rect branches, dark green, flattened, needle-like leaves. Cup-shaped, fleshy red fruit in winter.

Bulbs

Allium cristophii

○ △ Su VH ↧ 25-50cm ·· 15cm
Striking summer flowering bulb. Tall flower stem, on top of which is a large globe of star-shaped, purple flowers. Grey, hairy leaves, semi-erect.

Allium ursinum
Ransoms/Wild garlic

◗ △ Sp VH ↧ 30-45 cm ·· 30-45cm
Spring flowering, hardy bulb with broad, strap-like, bright green leaves that smell strongly of garlic if crushed. The flower spike is crowned with a cluster of small, starry-white flowers.

Anemone coronaria Windflower

○ △ Sp VH ↧ 15-45cm ·· 15cm
Spring flowering bulb. Parsley-like, semi-erect, divided leaves. Large, shallow, cup-shaped flower. Colour varies from white through blue to purple and red.

Bulbocodium vernum

○ △ Sp VH ↧ 3-4cm ·· 3-5cm
Spring-flowering corm. Reddish-purple, widely funnel-shaped, stemless flowers. Narrow leaves appear later, and die down in summer

Cardiocrinum giganteum
Giant lily

◗ ◗ Su VH ↧ 3m ·· 75-110cm
Stout, leafy stem topped with flowering spike of pendent, long, cream-white trumpets streaked purple-red inside.

Chinodoxa forbesii 'Pink Giant'
Glory-of-the-snow

○ △ Wi VH ↧ 15-20cm ·· 3cm
Winter flowering bulb with two semi-erect, narrow leaves. Flowering

stem produces spike of star-shaped, white-eyed, flat pink flowers.

Colchicum autumnale
Meadow saffron

○ △ Au VH ↧ 10-15cm ·· 10-15cm
Autumn flowering corm. Wine-glass-shaped, mauve flowers followed by large, strap-shaped leaves. 'Waterlily' has double flowers.

Crocosmia x crocosmiiflora 'George Davison' Montbretia

○ △ Su VH ↧ 60cm ·· 20cm
Vigorous, clump forming, mid to late summer flowering bulb. Sprays of yellow-orange, funnel-shaped flowers among dense clumps of narrow, sword-shaped leaves. Can be invasive.

Crocus sativus Saffron crocus

○ △ Au VH ↧ 15cm ·· 7.5cm
Autumn flowering corm. Narrow basal leaves appear with purple flowers with dark purple veining. Bright red stigmas yield saffron.

Crocus tommasinianus

○ △ Wi VH ↧ 7.5-10cm ·· 5cm
Late winter to early spring flowering corm. Slender, funnel-shaped flowers. Petals pale lilac to dark purple, orange centre. Leaves have white central vein.

Crocus vernus Dutch crocus

○ △ Sp VH ↧ 10cm ·· 5cm
Spring flowering corm. Goblet-shaped flowers, striped or in shades of white, purple or violet. Central stigma is orange or yellow. *C. v.* 'Purpureus Grandiflorus' has purple-blue flowers.

Cyclamen coum

◗ △ Wi VH ↧ 10cm ·· 5-10cm
Winter flowering tuber. Bright carmine flowers, darkly stained at mouth, rounded, deep green or silver patterned leaves appear either before, or at the same time as the flowers.

Dactylorhiza majalis
Western marsh orchid

○ △ Sp VH ↧ 75 cm ·· 25cm
Deciduous, terrestrial orchid. Long, lance-shaped green leaves, sometimes spotted pink. Pyramidal dense cluster of lilac to magenta tubular flowers with recurved lip.

Fritillaria meleagris
Snake's-head fritillary

○ ◗ Sp VH ↧ 30cm ·· 5-8cm
Slender, narrow, grey-green leaves.

Solitary bell-shaped, white or checkered purple pendent flower on slender stem.

Fritillaria pallidiflora Fritillary

○ △ Sp VH
↧ 30-45cm ·· 10-15cm
Lance-shaped, grey-green leaves in pairs. Bell-shaped, creamy yellow to greenish yellow flowers patterned brownish red within.

Galanthus nivalis
Common snowdrop

○ △ Wi VH ↧ 10-15cm ·· 5-7.5cm
Pendent white flowers on a slender stem in late winter. Large outer petals and smaller inner ones form an upside-down cup marked green. Narrow, semi-erect, strap-shaped, grey-green leaves.

Hyacinthoides non-scripta
English bluebell

◗ ◗ VH ↧ 25-35cm ·· 10-15cm
Tuft forming bulb. Bright green, upright leaves. Erect flower stem, arched at tip, with fragrant, tube-like, blue bells, the ends of which curl back at the mouth.

Hyacinthus orientalis
Hyacinth

○ △ Sp VH
↧ 20-30 cm ·· 7.5-10cm
Spring flowering, clump forming bulb. Semi-erect, wide, glossy leaves. Lax flowering spike with small, waxy, bell-shaped, very fragrant, pale blue flowers with recurved tips.

Iris flavescens 'Florentina' Orris

○ △ Sp VH ↧ 1m ·· indefinite
Spring flowering, bearded, intermittent iris with pale blue-white flowers the throats of which are delicate yellow. The leaves are sword-shaped, arching and narrow. This iris was the medieval emblem of the city of Florence.

Iris pallida Dalmatian iris

○ △ Sp VH ↧ 70cm-1m ·· indefinite
Rhizomatous iris. Large, lilac-blue, scented flowers with yellow beards in late spring and early summer. Long, arching, lance-shaped leaves.

Lilium candidum Madonna lily

○ △ >7 Su VH ↧ 1-2m ·· 20-25cm
Stiff flowering stem with narrow leaves, outward-facing, pure white, fragrant, trumpet-shaped flowers flaring widely at the mouth.

Lilium 'Connecticut King'

○ △ Su VH ↧ 1m ·· 20-25cm
A hybrid with upward-facing, cup-shaped, bright yellow flowers contrasting with narrow green leaves also borne on the upright stem.

Lilium monadelphum

○ △ Su VH ↧ 1-1.5m ·· 20-25cm
Stem has scattered, lance-shaped leaves and, at the top, nodding, scented, turkscap flowers, yellow with purple or deep red spots on the side.

Lilium pumilum

○ △ Su VH ↧ 25-60cm ·· 15-20cm
Stem has small, scattered, linear leaves and scented, flat, vivid scarlet turkscap flowers, some black spotted in centre.

Lilium pyrenaicum
Yellow turkscap lily

○ △ Sp VH
↧ 30cm-1.2m ·· 20-25cm
Stem has scattered, linear, hairless leaves and nodding, turkscap flowers unpleasantly scented. Long petals are green-yellow to yellow with deep purple lines and spots.

Lilium regale Regal lily

○ △ Su VH ↧ 1-1.8m ·· 15-20cm
Lily with linear leaves and fragrant, outward-facing, trumpet-shaped flowers. Long petals, white inside with yellow base, pink-purple outside with protruding golden anthers.

Narcissus 'Cheerfulness'

○ △ Sp VH ↧ 40cm ·· 15cm
Spring flowering daffodil. Fragrant, double white flowers with cream and yellow segments in the centre.

Narcissus pseudonarcissus
Lent lily

○ △ Sp VH ↧ 25-35cm ·· 5-10cm
Fragrant, usually solitary, nodding flower. Overlapping, straw yellow outer petals surround darker yellow trumpet flared at the mouth.

Narcissus 'Tête-à-Tête' Daffodil

○ △ Sp VH ↧ 15-20cm ·· 5cm
Dwarf, early flowering bulb. Long-lasting flowers, reflexed rich, golden-yellow petals, warm orange-yellow hexagonal trumpet. Arching leaves.

Nerine bowdenii 'Wellsii'
Guernsey lily

○ △ Au FH ⊕ 45-60cm · · 7.5-10cm
Strap-shaped, semi-erect basal leaves. Pink flowers with recurved tips. Needs a warm wall.

Orchis mascula
Early purple orchid

○ △ Sp VH ⊕ 20-40 cm · · 20cm
Terrestrial, deciduous orchid. Shiny, oblong, dark green leaves, often with purple blotches. Bright purple-crimson helmet-shaped flowers with drooping lip; smells of tom cat.

Tulipa humilis

○ △ Sp VH ⊕ 20cm · · 7.5-10cm
Early flowering species. Grey-green, slightly arching leaves, magenta-pink flowers with yellow centre.

Tulipa linifolia
Batalini Group 'Red Gem'

○ △ Sp VH ⊕ 10-15cm · · 10cm
Early flowering hybrid. Grey-green leaves. Orange-red flowers with purple-black centres.

Tulipa saxatilis Cretan tulip

○ △ Sp VH ⊕ 10-15cm · · 10cm
Early flowering species. Slightly arching, narrow, shiny green leaves. Scented, mid pink flowers yellow at the base. Needs very warm, sunny position.

Tulipa turkestanica

○ △ Sp VH ⊕ 10-30cm · · 10cm
Early flowering species. Grey-green leaves, hairy flowering stem. Flowers, with unpleasant odour, have oval, white petals flushed green or pink outside, orange-yellow centre.

Vanda dearei Orchid

◗ △ Su TT ⊕ 45cm · · 30cm
Epiphytic orchid. Flat, oblong, dull green leaves. Large, flat flowers, lemon-yellow or cream, brown veined and scented. V. tricolor has pink flowers.

Flowering Annuals and Perennials

Agrostemma githago
Corncockle

○ △ Su VH ⊕ 60cm-1m · · 30cm
Summer flowering, erect annual. Lance-shaped, mid green leaves, open, trumpet-shaped pink flowers. Grows best in poor soil. Seeds are poisonous.

Anemone x hybrida
Japanese anemone

○ △ Su VH
⊕ 1.2-1.5m · · 60-120cm
Vigorous, upright perennial. Deeply divided, dark green leaves, cup-shaped single flowers, white to bright pink, late summer to autumn. Can be invasive.

Anthurium andraeanum
Flamingo flower

◗ ◗ Su TT ⊕ 60-75cm · · 50cm
Evergreen, erect perennial. Oval, leathery, long stalked, dark green leaves. The flower is surrounded by heart-shaped, bright red, long lasting spathes.

Aquilegia canadensis
Canadian columbine

○ △ Su VH ⊕ 60-90cm · · 30-35cm
Clump forming, leafy perennial with dark green, fern-like foliage. In early summer, slender flowering stem bears bell-shaped, semi-pendent, lemon-yellow flowers with red spurs.

Aubrieta 'Purple Cascade'

○ △ Sp VH ⊕ 10cm · · 20cm
Trailing annual. Small, soft green leaves almost obscured by masses of purple-blue flowers in spring and summer.

Bellis perennis Common daisy

○ △ Sp VH ⊕ 10cm · · 10cm
Carpeting perennial with oval, mid green leaves. White, daisy flower in early spring. Often grows in lawns.

Campanula latiloba Bellflower

○ △ Su VH ⊕ 1m · · 45cm
Wiry flowering stem rises from a rosette of oval leaves bearing shallow, widely cup-shaped flowers in shades of blue, occasionally white or mauve-pink.

Convallaria majalis
Lily-of-the-valley

◗ ◗ Sp ⊕ 20-30cm · · 30-40cm
Deciduous, rhizomatous, low growing perennial with narrowly oval, mid to

dark green leaves. In late spring. pendulous, fragrant, white, bell-shaped flowers between a pair of leaves.

Convolvulus tricolor

○ △ Su VH ⊕ 20-30cm · · 20cm
Fast growing, bushy, upright annual with mid green, oval to lance-shaped leaves. Trumpet- to saucer-shaped, blue and white flowerss.

Delphinium elatum hybrids

○ △ Su VH
⊕ 1.35-2.2m · · 75cm-1m
Erect perennial. Large, palmate leaves with tall flowering spire of densely packed, individual flowers in a range of colours. 'Blue Nile', rich blue flowers streaked light blue, white eyes. 'Butterball', creamy eyed, white flowers. 'Mighty Atom', mid violet, yellow-brown or violet marked eyes.

Dianthus 'Haytor White' Pink

○ △ Su VH ⊕ 30cm · · 25-40cm
Evergreen, clump forming perennial. Silver-grey, narrow leaves. In mid summer, masses of double, pure white, fragrant flowers with fringed petals.

Dianthus gratianopolitanus
Cheddar Pink

○ △ Su VH ⊕ 10-25cm · · 25-40cm
Evergreen perennial that produces a mat of grey-green, narrow leaves. In mid summer, the slender stems carry very fragrant, single, pink flowers with a wavy fringe. Perfect plant for the rock garden.

Dianthus 'Musgrave's Pink'

○ △ Su VH ⊕ 25-45cm · · 25-35cm
One of the earliest hybrid pinks, dating from c.1730. Narrow, grey-green leaves and scented, single white flowers with a green eye and a frilly edge, in mid summer.

Dictamnus albus Burning bush

○ △ Su VH ⊕ 45-90cm · · 45-60cm
Upright perennial. Light green leaves divided into oval leaflets smelling of lemon when crushed. In summer, fragrant, white, star-shaped flowers with long stamens followed by star-shaped seed pods. D.s. var. purpureus has pink flowers.

Digitalis x mertonensis
Foxglove

◗ ◗ Sp VH ⊕ 75cm · · 30cm
Perennial with rosette of soft, hairy, oval leaves. Tall spires of tubular,

downward pointing flowers, bruised pink to copper-mauve in summer.

Epimedium x versicolor
'Neosulphureum'

◗ △ Sp VH ⊕ 30-35cm · · 30-60cm
Dense, carpeting perennial. Heart-shaped leaves tinted reddish purple in spring; fine autumn colour. Clusters of small, pale yellow, cup-shaped flowers.

Erysimum cheiri Wallflower

○ △ Sp VH ⊕ 25-30cm · · 30-40cm
Evergreen, bushy perennial usually grown as biennial. Short, lance-shaped, mid to deep green leaves. Heads of sweetly fragrant flowers, mainly orange and yellow, but they range from deep velvety red to white.

Geranium renardii

○ △ Su VH ⊕ 30cm · · 30cm
Compact, clump forming perennial. Sage-green, circular, lobed, velvety leaves. Flat white flowers, sometimes with purple veining, in early summer.

Geranium sanguineum
Bloody cranesbill

○ △ Su VH ⊕ 20-30cm · · 30-45cm
Spreading, hump forming perennial. Dark green, finely-cut leaves. In summer, covered with masses of bright magenta-pink, cup-shaped flowers with white eyes.

Geranium sylvaticum
'Mayflower' Wood cranesbill

◗ △ Su Vh ⊕ 1m · · 60cm
Upright, clump forming perennial with deeply lobed, soft, bright green, slightly aromatic leaves. Above the foliage rise branching stems of cup-shaped, violet-blue, white-eyed flowers in early summer.

Gypsophila paniculata
'Bristol Fairy' Baby's Breath

○ △ Su VH ⊕ 60-75cm · · 1m
Perennial with wiry, branching stems and masses of tiny, white, double flowers in summer. The leaves are small and dark green.

Hedychium coronarium
Butterfly lily

○ ◗ Su HH ⊕ 2m · · 60cm-1m
Upright perennial. Lance-shaped, mid green leaves which are downy beneath. The pyramidal flowering spike is densely packed with white, fragrant. butterfly-like flowers which are yellow blotched near the base.

Hemerocallis lilioasphodelus
Daylily

○ ◗ Sp VH ↕ 75-90cm ·· 75-90cm

Spreading, clump forming perennial. Narrow, sword-shaped, mid green leaves. Delicate, upright flowering spike with large, very fragrant, trumpet-shaped, lemon yellow flowers in late spring and early summer.

Hemerocallis 'Stafford'

○ ◗ Su VH ↕ 75cm ·· 60cm

Clump forming, vigorous perennial with strap-shaped, mid green leaves. Bright red, large, trumpet-shaped flowers with maroon and yellow throat with yellow mid rib on each petal.

Hesperis matronalis
Dame's violet, sweet rocket

○ △ Su VH ↕ 75cm ·· 60cm

Upright perennial. Smooth, narrowly oval leaves. Long, upright spikes of densely clustered, small, violet or white flowers give off a strong fragrance on summer evenings.

Inula helenium Elecampane

○ △ Su VH ↕ 3m ·· 60cm

Robust perennial with a thick, aromatic rhizome. Stout, branching, erect stem with tapering leaves up to 75cm in length. Produces a mass of daisy-like, bright yellow flowers.

Inula hookeri

○ △ Su VH ↕ 75cm ·· 45cm

Clump forming, upright perennial. Hairy, lance-shaped, bright green leaves. Masses of large, daisy-like, slightly scented, yellowish-green flowers with orange centre.

Iris, bearded

○ △ Su VH ↕ varies ·· indefinite

Rhizomatous spreading perennial. The group covers the majority of irises, distinct because the large flowers have 'beards' of numerous, often coloured hairs along the centre of the drooping petals ('fall'). 'Carnaby' (↕ 1m), in early summer, pale pink flowers with deep, rose-pink fall, orange beards. 'Early Light' (↕ 1m), cream-lemon fall, yellow beard. 'Flamenco' (↕ 1m), gold infused beard with red, white to yellow fall. 'Stepping Out' (↕ 1m), fall and beard deep purple with blue marks.

Kniphofia 'Erecta'
Red-hot poker

○ ○ Su VH

↕ 50-150cm ·· 60-75cm

Evergreen perennial. Coarse edged, upright, arching, narrow lance-shaped, blue-green leaves. Stout stem bears terminal spike of densely clustered red, upward-pointing florets in late summer, early autumn.

Lewisia rediviva Bitter root

○ △ <7 Sp VH ↕ 1-4cm ·· 5cm

Tufted, rosetted perennial. Large pink (or white) many-petalled flowers, late spring to early summer. Small, narrow leaves hidden by flowers in summer.

Lupinus perennis Sundial lupin

○ △ >7 Sp VH ↕ 60cm ·· 45cm

Perennial. Leaves with 8 narrow leaflets. Spikes of small blue, rarely pink or white flowers, from late spring to early summer.

Lychnis chalcedonica
Maltese cross

○ △ Su VH ↕ 90-120cm ·· 30-45cm

Neat. clump forming perennial. Mid green, slightly hairy leaves. Domed head of small, scarlet flowers with notched petals contrasting with foliage.

Lychnis flos-jovis
Flower of Jove

○ △ Su VH ↕ 45cm ·· 45cm

Clump forming perennial. Narrow, pointed, silver-grey foliage. Rounded clusters of deep purplish-pink flowers with notched petals.

Matthiola incana
Brompton stock

○ △ Su FH ↕ 30-60cm ·· 30cm

Upright, bushy, fast growing, short lived perennial usually grown as annual. Greyish-green leaves, light purple flowers.

Meconopsis betonicifolia
Himalayan blue poppy

● ◗ <7 Sp VH ↕ 1-1.2m ·· 45cm

Clump forming perennial. Hairs give a slight rusty tint to basal and stem leaves. In late spring, early summer, papery, bright purplish-blue flowers.

Myosotis sylvatica
Wood forget-me-not

○ △ Sp VH ↕ 45cm ·· 45cm

Perennial, usually grown as biennial. Dark green leaves with bristle-like hairs, clusters of small, pale blue, rarely white flowers, late spring and summer.

Oenothera biennis
Evening primrose

○ △ Su VH ↕ 1-1.2m ·· 30-45cm

Upright biennial that self-seeds easily and may become invasive. Oval, toothed leaves. Cup-shaped, primrose-yellow, silky flowers, sometimes fragrant, open in the evening.

Osteospermum 'Whirligig'
Sailor daisy

○ △ Su FH ↕ 60cm ·· 30-45cm

Evergreen, clump forming, prostrate perennial. Profusion of single white flowers with collar of florets like mini spoons. Leaves are grey-green.

Pachystachys lutea
Lollipop plant

◗ △ Su TT ↕ 1.2m ·· 1m

Evergreen, rounded, shrubby perennial with ovate, heavily veined leaves. Tall flower spike is four-sided due to arrangement of intensely yellow-gold, large oval bracts.

Paeonia lactiflora
'White Wings' Peony

○ △ Su VH ↕ 80cm ·· 60-120cm

Clump forming perennial with glossy, dark green leaves that colour in autumn. Masses of large, single, fragrant, white flowers with slightly ruffled petals, on red flower stalks.

Papaver rhoeas Field poppy

○ △ Su VH ↕ 60cm ·· 30cm

Fast growing annual with basal rosette of finely cut leaves. Single, delicate, paper-like, cup-shaped scarlet flowers.

Papaver somniferum
Opium poppy

○ △ Su VH ↕ 45-90cm ·· 60-90cm

Upright, fast growing annual. Light greyish-green, oblong leaves. Large single/double flowers with papery petals, red, pink, purple or white.

Pilosella aurantiaca
Fox-and-cubs

○ △ Su VH ↕ 30-45cm ·· 30cm

Mound forming, invasive perennial. Upright, slightly arching, oval, downy leaves. Dandelion-like orange-brown flowers on wiry stems.

Polygonatum odoratum
Angled Solomon's seal

● △ Sp VH ↕ 60cm ·· 30-45cm

Rhizomatous. arching perennial. Mid green leaflets, pairs of tubular to bell-shaped, fragrant, green-tipped

white flowers hang from underside of leaves. *P. x hybridum* (Solomon's seal), hybrid between *P. o.* and *P. multiflorum*. Ivory flowers, leaves veined, less arched.

Primula florindae
Giant cowslip

○ ◗ Su VH ↕ 60cm-1m ·· 30-60cm

The giant among primulas. Upright, bold, clump forming perennial. Tall stems crowned with ring of numerous lemon to sulphur yellow flowers in early to mid summer.

Primula veris Cowslip

○ ◗ Sp VH ↕ 15-20cm ·· 15-20cm

Clump forming perennial with oval to lance-shaped, mid green, toothed leaves. Clusters of fragrant, yellow, tubular flowers on a stout stem.

Primula vialii

○ ◗ Su VH ↕ 15-45cm ·· 23-30cm

Short-lived, clump forming perennial. Rosette of upright, hairy leaves. Dense conical spike with mauve florets open from scarlet calyces in late spring.

Primula vulgaris Primrose

○ ◗ Sp VH ↕ 15-20cm ·· 25-35cm

Neat, clump forming perennial. Rosette of bright green, lance-shaped, toothed leaves. In early spring, clusters of soft yellow flowers on delicate stalks.

Pulsatilla vulgaris
Pasque flower

○ △ Sp VH ↕ 15-23cm ·· 15-23cm

Nodding, cup-shaped, lilac or white flowers with golden anthers above the ferny tufts of feathery, soft, hairy leaves, followed by feathery seed heads.

Silene dioica Red campion

○ △ Sp VH ↕ 30-45cm ·· 23-30cm

Somewhat leggy and untidy annual. Upright, arching stems with oval, mid green leaves. Clusters of bright pink flowers. *S. d. alba* has white flowers.

Stokesia laevis Stokes' aster

○ △ Su VH ↕ 30-45cm ·· 30-45cm

Perennial with over-wintering rosette of leaves. White cornflower-like flowers on the top of stems. Pointed leaves with white mid vein.

Thermopsis villosa
Carolina lupin

○ △ Su VH ↕ 1m ·· 60cm

A straggling perennial with glaucous

leaves divided into three oval leaflets. In late summer, long stems have racemes of yellow, pea-like flowers.

Trillium grandiflorum
White wake robin

● ◗ Sp VH ⫶ 30-45cm ·· 30-45cm

Clump forming perennial. Large, pure white, triangular-shaped flowers with yellow centres above mound of dark green, arrow-shaped leaves.

Veronica chamaedrys
Germander speedwell

○ ◌ Su VH ⫶ 25cm ·· 20cm

Rhizomatous perennial. Upright, branching stems. Grey-green leaves oval and slightly hairy. Short flowering spike bearing small blue flowers with white throat in late spring and summer.

Veronica spicata
Spiked speedwell

○ ◌ Su VH ⫶ 60-80cm ·· 15-30cm

Clump forming perennial. Narrow, oval, toothed, mid green leaves. Small flowering stems produce spikes of small, star-shaped. bright blue flowers. The whole plant is covered with small, silver hairs.

Vicia cracca Tufted vetch

○ ◌ Sp VH ⫶ 30-120cm ·· 30cm

Small, oblong leaflets with terminal tendril. Flowers, small, pea-like, deep purple, borne along a flowering stalk.

Viola cornuta 'Alba'
White horned violet

○ ◌ Su VH ⫶ 12-20 cm ·· 20cm

Rhizomatous perennial. Toothed, oval, bright green leaves. Early to late summer, erect flower stalks with white, angular, flat-faced, spurred flowers. Also pale to deep lilac form.

Viola odorata Sweet violet

○ ◌ Wi VH ⫶ 10-15cm ·· 30-45cm

Semi-evergreen, stoloniferous, spreading perennial. Toothed, heart-shaped leaves. Flat-faced, sweetly scented, blue or white flower, from late winter to mid spring.

Viola tricolor Heartsease

○ ◌ Sp VH ⫶ 5-15cm ·· 5-15cm

Short lived perennial often grown as annual. Short, arrow-shaped leaves, flat-faced flowers in combinations of yellow, white and shades of purple. Will go on flowering until autumn.

Flowering Shrubs

Abelia x grandiflora

○ ◌ Su VH ⫶ 3m ·· 3m

Vigorous, branched, medium-sized, semi-evergreen shrub. Dark, glossy green foliage, arching habit. Masses of scented, star-shaped, pink-tinged, white flowers from mid summer to autumn.

Allamanda 'Golden Sprite'

○ ◌ Su TT ⫶ 1m ·· 3ft 1m

Small, compact shrub with glossy, leathery light green, evergreen foliage. Small, brilliant yellow flowers, chocolate brown in bud, all year round.

Artemisia arborescens
Wormwood

○ ◌ Su HH ⫶ 1.5m ·· 75cm

Upright, evergreen shrub. Soft, silver-white, finely cut, aromatic foliage. Small, grey-green flowers with yellow-brown centres, late summer to autumn.

Buddleja davidii 'Black Knight'
Butterfly bush

○ ◌ Su VH ⫶ 2.5-3.7m ·· 2.5-3.7m

Deciduous, vigorous, arching shrub. Long, deep green, lance-shaped leaves, white felted beneath. Plumes of tiny, tubular, dark violet-purple flowers mid summer to autumn.

Camellia japonica 'Tricolor'

◗ ◌ <7 Sp FH ⫶ 3-6m ·· 3-4.5m

Compact evergreen shrub. Glossy, dark green, oval leaves. This cultivar has semi-double, medium-sized white flowers, streaked with carmine.

Camellia sasanqua

◗ ◌ <7 Au VH ⫶ 3-6m ·· 3-4.5m

Dense, upright, fast growing evergreen shrub. Long, oval-shaped, bright green leaves. This species is a little unusual, and bears a profusion of flatish to cup-shaped, single, fragrant, white flowers in the autumn.

Camellia x williamsii 'Donation'

◗ ◌ <7 Sp VH

⫶ 1.8-4.5m ·· 90cm-3m

Evergreen, upright, spreading shrub with small, glossy, mid green leaves. In spring, bush is cloaked with a mass of semi-double, cup-shaped, pink flowers.

Carpenteria californica
Tree anemone

○ ◗ Su FH ⫶ 2m ·· 2m

Evergreen, domed, bushy shrub. Lance-shaped, dark green, glossy leaves and white, fragrant, yellow-centred, camellia-like flowers all summer long.

Chimonanthus praecox
Wintersweet

○ ◌ Wi VH ⫶ 2.5m ·· 3m

Bushy, deciduous shrub. In winter, bare branches covered with stalkless, almost translucent-yellow, scented flowers. Roughly oval, glossy, dark green leaves.

Cistus salviifolius Rock rose

○ ◌ Su VH ⫶ .75m ·· 0.75m

Dense, bushy evergreen shrub. Grey-green, wrinkled foliage forming a dome shape. Masses of white, cup-shaped flowers with central yellow blotches throughout early summer.

Cistus x cyprius

○ ◌ Su VH ⫶ 1.5m ·· 1.5m

Bushy, evergreen shrub with glossy, dark green, narrow, sticky leaves. Large, white flowers with a yellow centre and red blotch at the base of each petal are borne in early summer.

Correa 'Mannii'
Australian fuchsia

○ ◌ Su FH ⫶ 2m ·· 2m

Bushy, slender-stemmed, evergreen shrub. Oval, narrow leaves, slightly hairy beneath. Tubular, scarlet, hanging flowers appear intermittently from late summer to spring.

Daphne mezereum Mezereon

○ ◌ Wi VH ⫶ 1.2m ·· 90-120cm

Upright, deciduous shrub. Fragrant, small, pink or purple flowers smother bare stems in winter, followed by red fleshy berries, dull, grey-green leaves.

Daphne odora 'Aureomarginata'

○ ◌ Wi VH ⫶ 1.5-1.8m ·· 1.5-1.8m

Bushy, evergreen shrub with dark green, oval leaves narrowly edged with yellow. From mid winter to early spring, tight clusters of fragrant, starry flowers appear at the tips of the stems.

Daphne x burkwoodii 'Astrid'

○ ◌ Sp VH ⫶ 1.5m ·· 1.5m

Upright, bushy, semi-evergreen shrub. Clusters of fragrant white and pink flowers in spring, occasionally second flowering in autumn. Mid green, lance-shaped leaves edged creamy white.

Euonymus europaeus Spindle

○ ◌ Au VH ⫶ 1.8-3m ·· 1.8-3m

Bushy, deciduous shrub. Mid green, narrow, oval leaves turn red in autumn. Spectacular purplish-pink autumnal fruit split to reveal orange seed coats.

Fothergilla major
Large fothergilla

◗ ◗ <7 Sp VH ⫶ 1.8-2.5m

·· 1.2-1.8m

Deciduous, upright shrub. Fragrant, bottle-brush tufts of white flowers on bare stems in spring. Glossy, dark green, oval leaves turn scarlet and orange in autumn.

Grevillea rosmarinifolia

○ ◌ <7 Su HH ⫶ 2m ·· 2m

Rounded, well branched evergreen shrub. Dense clusters of tubular, red flowers. Dark green leaves, silky haired beneath, shaped like those of rosemary.

Halimium 'Susan'

○ ◌ Su FH ⫶ 45cm ·· 60cm

Small, spreading, evergreen shrub. Dark green, fairly small, oval leaves. Bright yellow cup-shaped flowers with prominent filament-like yellow anthers. May become invasive.

Hamamelis mollis
Chinese witch hazel

○ ◌ Wi VH ⫶ 4m ·· 4m

Deciduous, open, upright shrub. In winter, fragrant yellow, spider-like flowers on bare branches. Oval, mid green leaves turn red, orange and yellow in autumn.

Heliotropium arborescens
Heliotrope

○ ◌ Sp TT ⫶ 75cm ·· 90cm

Bushy, evergreen shrub. Finely wrinkled, semi-glossy, dark green leaves. Flat clusters of slightly scented purple to white flowers from late spring until winter.

Hypericum androsaemum
Tutsan

◗ ◌ Su VH ⫶ 75cm ·· .75m

Deciduous shrub with oval, rich green leaves. Small, star-shaped, yellow flowers, followed by round black berries in autumn.

Kalmia latifolia Calico bush

○ ▶ <7 Su VH ⌇ 3m · · 3m
Evergreen, bushy, dense shrub.
Leathery, dark green leaves, almost
obscured by large clusters of pink,
bowl-shaped flowers.

Mahonia aquifolium 'Apollo'
Oregon grape

▶ ▶ Sp VH ⌇ 90cm-120cm · · 1.5m
Evergreen, open shrub. Leaves of bright
green, glossy leaflets often turn purple
and red in winter. Large clusters of
bright yellow flowers, followed by
grape-like blue-black berries.

Philadelphus x *temoisei*
'Erectus' Mock orange

○ △ Su VH ⌇ 1.2-1.5m · · 1.2-1.5
Deciduous, open branched shrub.
Oval, dark green leaves, masses of
fragrant white flowers.

Potentilla fruticosa 'Red Ace'

▶ △ Sp VH ⌇ 0.75m · · 1.5m
Spreading, dense, bushy, deciduous
shrub. Narrow, compact, lance-shaped,
grey-green to dark green leaves. Bright
vermilion flowers with yellow centres,
from late spring to mid autumn.

Rhododendron 'Elizabeth'

▶ △ <7 Sp VH ⌇ 1.5-4m · · 1.5-4m
Evergreen, dome-shaped. Oblong leaves
and trusses of large, brilliant red,
trumpet-shaped flowers.

Rhododendron falconeri

▶ ▶ <7 Sp FH ⌇ 7.5-12m · · 3-6m
Evergreen, upright, large shrub with
cinnamon-coloured bark, long, deep
green, leathery leaves with yellowy
veins, orange beneath. Large trusses of
creamy yellow, bell-shaped flowers
marked purple inside.

Rhododendron luteum Azalea

▶ ▶ <7 Sp VH ⌇ 2.5-3.7m · · 2.2-3m
Deciduous shrub with open habit.
Masses of funnel-shaped, bright yellow,
richly fragrant flowers. Oblong, lance-
shaped leaves colour richly in autumn.

Rosa 'Aloha'

○ △ VH ⌇ 2.5m · · 2.5m
Stiff, bushy climbing rose. Leaves
leathery, dark green. Large, cup-shaped,
fully double, fragrant rose- and salmon-
pink flowers, late summer and autumn.

Rosa x *damascena*
Damask rose

○ △ Su VH ⌇ 2m ⌇ 3m
Small shrub with greyish-green leaves.
Large, fragrant flowers, red to white,
followed by white hips. *R. d.* var.
versicolor, unusual form with loosely
double, white flowers irregularly flaked
pink or blotched rose-red.

Rosa gallica var. *officinalis*
Apothecary's rose

○ △ VH ⌇ 75cm · · 1m
Old, well loved rose. Neat, bushy habit,
dark green leaflets. Masses of richly
fragrant, semi-double, rosy-crimson
flowers with prominent yellow anthers.

Rosa hemisphaerica
Sulphur rose

○ △ Su VH ⌇ 2m · · 1.2m
Medium-sized shrub with sea-green
leaflets. Sweetly scented, double
flowers, sulphur yellow, throughout
the summer.

Rosa 'Madame Hardy'

○ △ Su VH ⌇ 1.5m · · 1.2m
Vigorous, upright, damask rose.
Leathery, mat green leaves. Richly
scented, fully double white flowers.

Rosa moschata
Musk rose

○ △ Su FH ⌇ 2-3.5m · · 1.2m
Vigorous, somewhat lax shrub. Glossy,
dark green leaflets. Late summer to
autumn, large flowerheads with musk
scented, creamy-white flowers.

Rosa rubiginosa
Eglantine/Sweet briar

○ △ Su VH ⌇ 2.4m · · 2.4m
Vigorous, arching thorny branches
with apple-scented foliage. Clear-pink
flowers in summer. In autumn, oval
hips turn bright red.

Rosa virginiana

○ △ Su VH ⌇ 1m · · 75cm
Small, suckering shrub. Glossy green
leaves turn purple, then crimson and
yellow in autumn. Bright pink flowers.

Telopea speciosissima
Waratah

○ △ >7 Su HH ⌇ 3m · · 2m
Bushy, erect evergreen shrub. Coarse,
serrated, oval leaves. Large showy
flowerhead has bright red, petal-like
bracts surrounding the small,
tubular red flowers.

Viburnum carlesii
Korean spice viburnum

○ △ Sp VH ⌇ 1.5-1.8m · · 1.8m
Rounded, deciduous, bushy shrub
with dark green leaves which turn red
in autumn. Pink buds open to scented,
white-and-pink flowers, followed by
black fruit.

Viburnum tinus Laurustinus

○ △ Wi VH ⌇ 2.5-3.7m · · 3m
Dense, evergreen, bushy shrub. Oval,
dark green leaves. Flat heads of small
white flowers from late winter through
spring, followed by blue-black fruit.

Viburnum x *bodnantense*
'Dawn'

○ △ Wi VH ⌇ 2.5-3.7m · · 1.5-2.5m
Upright, deciduous, shrub. Oval leaves
bronzy at first, later bright green.
Clusters of deep pink buds open to
very fragrant pink flowers, from late
autumn to early spring.

Water Plants and Marginals

Carex elata 'Aurea'
Bowles' golden sedge

○ ◆ VH ⌇ 50-70cm · · 40-50cm
Tuft forming, evergreen perennial sedge
with narrow, upright and arching,
bright golden-yellow leaves with
narrow green margins. Browny-black
flower spikes in summer.

Iris pseudacorus Yellow flag

● ◆ Su VH ⌇ 2m · · 30-45cm
Vigorous beardless iris. Broad, ridged,
greyish-green, sword-like leaves.
Branched stem with yellow-gold
flowers, often brown or violet veining.

Matteuccia struthiopteris
Ostrich-feather fern/
Shuttlecock fern

▶ ◆ VH ⌇ 1-1.5m · · 60-90cm
Deciduous, rhizomatous fern with
outer rim of gently arching, yellow-
green fronds, inside which are shorter
greenish brown fronds. Both sets spear-
shaped, very thin and deeply cut with
blackish-brown mid ribs.

Nymphaea 'American Star'
Water lily

○ Su VH · · 1.2m
Deciduous perennial with heart-shaped,
floating leaves purple-bronze when
young becoming bright green.
Throughout the summer, deep pink,
star-shaped, semi-double flowers held
above the water.

Nymphaea nouchali var.
caerulea Blue water lily

○ Su TT · · 1.2m
Bright green, heart-shaped leaves and
many-petalled flowers. Each petal is
light blue at the tip shading to purple at
the base. Flower centre is deep yellow.

Nymphaea 'Marliacea Albida'
Water lily

○ Su VH · · 2m
Deciduous perennial with deep green,
heart-shaped leaves with purple-green
undersides. Pure white, cup-shaped,
semi-double fragrant flowers are
produced in summer.

Osmunda regalis Royal fern

▶ ◆ VH ⌇ 2m · · 1m
Deciduous fern with broadly triangular,
divided, bright green fronds, pinkish
when young. Mature plants have rust-
brown, tassel-like flower spikes at the
end of taller fronds.

index

acknowledgments

Key: **p** = page, **t** = top, **c** = centre, **b** = bottom, **l** = left, **r** = right, GPL = Garden Picture Library, des = designer

Front and back endpapers Jerry Harpur/des: Thomas Church, **p1** GPL/Lamontagne, **p2** GPL/Gary Rogers, **p3** Melanie Eclare, **p4/5** GPL/Steven Wooster, **p6/7** Tim Street-Porter/Galuez/Baragán, **p8** Jerry Harpur/des: Tom Hobbs, **p9 t** GPL/Gary Rogers, c Hugh Palmer/Polly Park, b GPL/Ron Sutherland, **p10** Jerry Harpur/Jean-Pierre Chalon, **p11** GPL/Steven Wooster, **p12/13** Jerry Harpur/des: Penelope Hobhouse, **p13 r** Steven Wooster, **p14/15** GPL/Michael Paul, **p16** Jerry Harpur/Crowinshield, USA, **p17 t** Bridgeman Art Library/Waterhouse and Dodd, London, b Jerry Harpur/Crowinshield, USA, **p18 t** GPL/Gary Rogers, b Jerry Harpur/des: Christopher Masson, London, **p20 t** Bridgeman Art Library/Victoria and Albert Museum, London, c GPL/Marijke Heuff, b Jerry Harpur/Daniel Baneuil, **p21** Hugh Palmer/Casa de Pilatos, **p23** The Interior Archive/Simon Upton/des:Grazia Gazzoni, **p24** Bridgeman Art Library/Osterreichische Nationalbibliothek, Vienna, **p25** Melanie Eclare/Les Jardins du Prieuré Notre Dame d'Orsan, France, **p26** Hugh Palmer/ Les Jardins du Prieuré Notre Dame d'Orsan, France, **p28** Jerry Harpur/Ilford Manor, **p29 t** Hugh Palmer/Isola Bella, Italy, **p29** b Marcus Harpur/Barnard's, Essex, **p30** The National Trust Picture Library, **p32 t** Bridgeman Art Library/Chester Beatty Library and Gallery of Oriental Art, Dublin, b GPL/Michael Paul, **p33** GPL/Steven Wooster, **p34 t** GPL/Michael Paul, bl GPL/Michael Paul, br GPL/Ron Sutherland, **p36** GPL/Gary Rogers, **p37 t** GPL/Steven Wooster, b Bridgeman Art Library/Museum of the City of New York, **p38** l GPL/Steven Wooster, tr GPL/Gary Rogers, br GPL/Gary Rogers, **p40** l GPL/Brigitte Thomas, r Bridgeman Art Library/Mallet and Son Antiques Ltd, London, **p41** Hugh Palmer/Jenkyn Place, **p42 t** GPL/Brigitte Thomas, b Hugh Palmer/Trewithin, **p44/45** Tim Street-Porter/Gilardi, **p45** tr Bridgeman Art Library/tr Bridgeman Art Library/© Fernando Botero, courtesy, Marlborough Gallery, New York, cr GPL/Michael Paul, br The Interior Archive/Cecilia Innes/José Yturbe, **p47** l Tim Street-Porter/Kahlo, tr The Interior Archive/Juan Sordo Madelena, br GPL/Gary Rogers, **p48** l Jerry Harpur/des: Thomas Church, r GPL/Vivian Russell, **p49** Jerry Harpur/des: Thomas Church, **p51 t** Jerry Harpur/des: Juan Grimm, b John Brookes Landscape Design/des: John Brookes **p52** Jerry Harpur/des: Topher Delaney, San Francisco, **p53 t** Jerry Harpur/des: Topher Delaney, San Francisco b Jerry Harpur/des: Steve Oliver, **p54** l Clive Nichols/des: Christopher Bradley-Hole, r GPL/Steven Wooster, **p56/57** GPL/Gary Rogers, **p58/59** GPL/Gary Rogers, **p59** r GPL/Jerry Pavia, **p60 t** GPL/Jerry Pavia, b GPL/Gary Rogers, **p62** GPL/Gary Rogers, **p63** Caroline Jones, **p65 t** GPL/Gary Rogers, b Jerry Harpur, **p67** GPL/Steven Wooster, **p69 t** GPL/Michael Paul, b GPL/Steven Wooster, **p70** Steven Wooster/Hampton Court Flower Show/des: Bonita Bulaitis, **p71** Melanie Eclare, **p72 t** Helen Fickling/des: Diana Yakeley, b Jerry Harpur/des: Tom Hobbs, **p74 t** GPL/Ron Sutherland, c Jerry Harpur/Sun House, Long Melford, Suffolk, **p75** Clive Nichols/Sue Berger, **p76 t** Hugh Palmer/Tyninghame House, East Linton, Lothian, c Helen Fickling/des: Diana Yakeley, b Helen Fickling/des: Ruth Barclay, **p78/79** GPL/Ron Sutherland, **p81 t** Clive Nichols/Simon Irvine, b The Interior Archive/Helen Fickling/des:Catherine Mason, **p82 t** GPL/Jerry Pavia, b GPL/Jacqui Hurst, **p84** GPL/Gary Rogers, **p85** Tim Street-Porter/Galuez/Baragán, **p86 t** Jerry Harpur, bl GPL/Michael Paul, br GPL/Gary Rogers, **p87 t** GPL/Ron Sutherland, b GPL/Gary Rogers, **p90/91** Melanie Eclare/des: Michele Osborne, **p90** l GPL/Ron Sutherland, r GPL/Michael Paul, **p92** l GPL/Steven Wooster/des: Michele Osborne, r GPL/Michael Paul, **p94/95** The Interior Archive/Simon Upton/des: Marja Walters/Michael Reeves, **p96 t** Clive Nichols/George Carter/Chelsea '99, b Steven Wooster/The Morrell's Garden, Wainui Beach, NZ, **p97** Arcaid/Garry Sarre/Belle, **p98/99** Jerry Harpur/des: Sonny Garcia, San Francisco, USA, **p98 tl** Jerry Harpur/des: Margot Knox, Melbourne, Aus., **p99 r** Jerry Harpur/des: Steve Chase, Palm Springs, USA, **p100 t** Jerry Harpur/des: Topher Delaney, San Francisco, b GPL/Marijke Heuff, **p101** Clive Nichols/des: Christopher Bradley-Hole, **p102 tl** GPL/Michael Paul, bc GPL/Gary Rogers, br Jerry Harpur/des: Stephen Woodhams, **p103** l Clive Nichols/des: Steve Bird, r GPL/John Glover, **p104** Jerry Harpur/des: Robert Watson, **p105** The Interior Archive/Simon Upton/des: Grazia Gazzoni, **p106** Jerry Harpur/Ryoan-ji Temple, Kyoto, **p107** Helen Fickling/des: Ruth Barclay, **p108 cl** The InteriorArchive/Herbert Ypma/José Yturbe, bl GPL/Michael Paul, r GPL/John Glover, **p109 t** Jerry Harpur, b GPL/Michael Paul, **p110/111** Jerry Harpur/des: Paul Guest, **p110 tl** GPL/Steven Wooster, bl GPL/Gil Hanly, **p111** tr Helen Fickling/Anne Birnhak, br GPL/Ron Sutherland, **p112/113** GPL/Steven Wooster, **p112 tl** GPL/Marijke Heuff, **p114** Jerry Harpur/Ilford Manor, **p115** Jerry Harpur/des: D Gabouland, **p116** Steven Wooster/Ross & Paula Greenville, **p117** GPL/Ron Sutherland, **p118/119** Jerry Harpur/des: R David Adams, **p118 t** Helen Fickling/des: Anne Birnhak, l Helen Fickling/des: Ruth Barclay, **p119 t** Jerry Harpur/des: Topher Delaney, San Francisco, **p119 r** Jerry Harpur/des: Claude & Andrez Dancel, **p120/121** Clive Nichols/Trevyn McDowell, **p120 t** Steven Wooster/des: Michele Osborne, bl Clive Nichols/des: Helen Sinclair & Mike Cedar, **p122/123** The Interior Archive/Fritz von der Schulenburg/des: Nico Rensch, **p124** l Helen Fickling/des: Ruth Barclay, r Helen Fickling/des: Ruth Barclay, **p125** Jerry Harpur/des: Annie Wilkes, **p126** Hugh Palmer, **p127** tl Helen Fickling/des: Diana Yakeley, tr Helen Fickling/des: Ruth Barclay, bl Clive Nichols/Robin Green/Ralph Cade, br Hugh Palmer/Kingstone Cottage, **p128** Terragram Pty Ltd/Walter Glover, **p129 t** Andrew Lawson/des: Jane Sweetser, Hampton Court '99, b Terragram Pty Ltd/Walter Glover, **p130** GPL/Gary Rogers, **p131** l GPL/Gary Rogers, r Melanie Eclare/des: Gunilla Pickard, **p132 t** Hugh Palmer, b GPL/John Neubauer, **p133** l Helen Fickling/des: Ruth Barclay, tr GPL/Steven Wooster, br Tim Street-Porter/Gilardi, **p134/135** Steven Wooster/James Wright's Garden nr. Aukland, NZ, **p134** l GPL/J.S. Sira, **p136** The Interior Archive/Tim Beddow, **p137** GPL/Gary Rogers, **p138** Hugh Palmer/Pelham Crescent, **p139 t** GPL/Michael Paul, b Helen Fickling/des: Diana Yakeley, **p140** l GPL/Brigitte Thomas, tr GPL/Steven Wooster, br GPL/Ron Sutherland, **p141** l Jerry Harpur/Jean Anderson, Seattle, USA, tr Jerry Harpur/des: Thomas Church, br Arcaid/Alan Weintraub, **p142** Helen Fickling/des: Anne Birnhak.

author's acknowledgments

I would like to thank everyone who has worked so hard and unceasingly to make this book a reality, especially Emily Hedges, Casey Horton, Erica Hunningher, Chris Gardner, Fiona Lindsay, Tony Lord, Larraine Shamwana, Jacqui Small, Helen Smythe, Arlene Sobel and Maggie Town. A great thank you is also due to my family and friends who have been so supportive and, of course, to Terry the Cat.

Toby Musgrave's Web site is at www:tobymusgrave.com

Note: While the instructions in this book are believed to be accurate and true at the time of going to press, they cannot replace the advice of specialists in appropriate cases. Therefore the author cannot accept any legal responsibility or liability for any loss, damage or injury caused by reliance on the accuracy of such instructions.